THE SPIRIT AND THE WORLD

Other Books by James W. Jones

The Shattered Synthesis:
New England Puritanism
before the Great Awakening

Filled with New Wine:
The Charismatic Renewal
of the Church

THE
SPIRIT
AND THE
WORLD

James W. Jones

HAWTHORN BOOKS, INC.
Publishers / NEW YORK

To Carey

•

THE SPIRIT AND THE WORLD

Library of Congress Catalog Card Number: 75-2557
ISBN: 0-8015-7034-4
1 2 3 4 5 6 7 8 9 10

Contents

Contents

Preface

The research behind these essays began while I was a
student, long before I encountered the charismatic
movement. A year in Minnesota, in which Sandra and I
became involved with several hundred people in a
charismatic community and where I became acquainted
with student communes, awakened my interest in community. Offers to give retreats and lectures on the topic of
Christian community nourished and refined my ideas.
Davis Yeuell, Theodore McConnell, and William Gentz
patiently read the manuscript and tried to teach me the fine
art of translating scholar's work into publishable form. In
the process they drew out of me a better book than I knew
was there. Eve Johnson's enthusiasm and hard work at the
typewriter saw the script through several revisions. To
Carey, whose life began simultaneously with that of this
Look and who will always remind her father that the Spirit
comes embodied in a variety of human forms, this work is
dedicated.

THE
SPIRIT
AND THE
WORLD

Introduction:
A New Charismatic Theology

American Christianity is rediscovering the Holy Spirit. A Protestant leader of the last decade predicted that this would be an era of the Spirit; the late Pope John prayed for a new Pentecost. Denominations pass resolutions about spirituality; parishes form adult groups to discuss prayer. Seminary students seek courses on the spiritual life; theologians hold conferences on the topic of religious experience. Some turn toward the East and try to adapt the techniques of yoga or transcendental meditation for use in the church. Among the most potent forces in this rediscovery of the Spirit is the Pentecostal movement. Begun at the turn of the century as a persecuted offshoot of American evangelicalism, Pentecostal denominations are the fastest-growing Christian bodies in the world. Their emphasis on the believers' direct experience of the Holy Spirit has infiltrated almost all the major Christian churches. By sheer enthusiasm and rate of growth these charismatics have forced denominations to take notice of them until now many—for example, the Lutherans,

Presbyterians, and Roman Catholics—have special commissions and organizations to study and often to promote charismatic spirituality.

None of this is really new. From the day of Pentecost Christians have sought to deepen their encounter with the Spirit and to increase their understanding of him. The history of the church is not one strand of development binding us to Jesus by a single cord but is rather a complex tapestry woven from many threads and with many loose ends around the edges. Many of these various strands and loose ends of Christian history have been movements that sought a deeper life in the Spirit: the montanists, followers of a second-century prophet, who protested the dying out of the ecstatic manifestations of the Spirit in the church; the great mystics of the Spanish middle ages, John of the Cross and Theresa of Ávila, and that humble follower of the Spirit, St. Francis of Assisi; the fiery spiritualists of seventeenth-century England, the Levellers, the Quakers, the Diggers, Ranters, and Seekers, who fashioned their experience of the Spirit into political revolution during the English civil war; the quiet spiritualists of the German Pietist movement, who translated their experience of the Spirit into an intense inward emotion; the modern Pentecostals, who have sprung unbidden into the life of the contemporary church.

What may be new in the modern thrust after the Spirit is a loss of balance between experience and reflection. The New Testament and the writings of the church fathers reveal that the early church not only experienced but thought about the Spirit. St. Paul, who exercised more charismatic gifts than even the superspiritual church of Corinth, transcribed his experience into letters that even his contemporaries said were heavy and hard to understand.

The fathers of the church put their philosophical training at the service of their spiritual experience. St. John and St. Theresa wrote treatises on mystical theology, which continue to inspire. The Quakers, through diaries, letters, and occasional pamphlets, preserved their understanding of the Spirit. And the German Pietists produced works of devotional theology that still live in the church life of the Continent. The present drive after spiritual experience often seems devoid of reflection. People appear in the mood to experience but not always in a mood to reflect upon that experience. A new encounter with the Spirit is rarely allowed to break apart old categories and free the Spirit to give rise to a new understanding.

One book will not solve this problem, but it can make a start. As a prologue to a new charismatic theology, this work sketches areas that need attention, questions that may be encountered, and directions that such a theology might take. Part of the analysis and background that are necessary resources for any contemporary theology of the Spirit are provided. Concerned with the Holy Spirit in the world today, it delineates some of the forms the Spirit is taking now, ways these new forms can be understood, and their implications for the church and the society. What follows is not only for charismatics, although many of my examples are drawn from this movement, in which I am involved. The areas discussed and the problems unveiled are not limited to any type of Christianity; they are the basic problems of encountering God, understanding that encounter, and relating it to the world in which we live.

St. Paul says the primary work of the Spirit is creating community among Christians. Simultaneous with the reawakening of interest in the Spirit, America developed a thirst after community. In the late sixties, cells of young people grouped themselves into communes, proclaiming the necessity of community. It was a proclamation the church should have been making—or at least listening to. This propulsion toward community on the part of the young might teach the church something of the nature of community and the importance of community to the Christian faith: a theme not much discussed in the Christian dogmatics of the nineteenth and early twentieth centuries. The communards of the sixties had a thirst for community but, like so many movements in the modern age, they refused to reflect deeply upon the forces that gave them birth and so were often unable to translate their ideas into viable communities. Both the rationale and the experience of community eluded them. A theology of community reveals why community often remains beyond the reach of communal movements and what is concretely involved in the formation of community.

At the same time this search for community was going on, sectors of the charismatic movement were recovering Paul's view of the Spirit as the creator of community. Especially among Roman Catholics and young Jesus people a new sensitivity to the Spirit walked hand in hand with a new impetus toward community. This book begins with the Spirit's activity in creating community. For St. Paul, community is a major part of the Spirit's work and so a theology of community is also a theology of the Spirit and a complete theology of the Spirit must discuss the nature of community.

Taking as a key to understanding the Holy Spirit Paul's focus on the Spirit in community, several issues are considered in this light. Beside the problem of community itself, discussed in the first chapter, is the dilemma of translating the intensity of the Spirit's work, traditionally associated with individual believers, into concern for the world. Probably no controversy has so torn the churches of modern America and so lastingly damaged them institutionally as the controversy over how to actively express God's love for his world. From the Civil War to the war in Vietnam churches have themselves been scenes of battle over the extent to which they should involve themselves in the sociopolitical problems of the day.

A major aspect of Jesus' teachings and an important element in discussing Christianity's responsibility for society is the concept of the Kingdom of God. A person's idea of the Kingdom of God shapes his idea of the church's role in society. If the Kingdom is defined as a political reality then political action to achieve it is a Christian imperative. If the Kingdom is defined in a more mystical sense then political action is irrelevant to it. The varieties of social ethics that have sprung up in America have all taken their start from some idea about the Kingdom. A theology of the Spirit in community gives us a new theology of the Kingdom and chapter 2 outlines how this theology gives new insight into the relation between the Gospel and the world.

From the beginning the experience of the Spirit created problems for the mind of the church. The church has never been content to simply experience the Spirit through religious ecstasy, community, or moral responsibility. Christians have also been concerned to conceptualize this experience in order to understand and communicate it, and so the church has developed a history of thought about the Spirit as well as a legacy of experience of the Spirit. This history shapes any contemporary attempt at a theology of the Spirit and must be confronted before any new theology can be done.

The period most influential in forming the church's

definition of the Spirit was the time of the New Testament community. Attempting to comprehend its experience of the Spirit with the forms of its culture, the New Testament church drew on both Greek philosophy and Hebrew religion. The difference between the ideas of these two groups created tensions in the New Testament picture of the Spirit, which subsequent generations inherited. Christians in the present have difficulties in understanding the Spirit and being open to a new theology of the Spirit because of this inheritance from the past. The historical process, which has passed its questions and inconsistencies on to the present, is summarized at the beginning of chapter 3. For the reader who is interested in a detailed analysis of the development of the church's thinking about the Spirit, further discussion is provided in chapter 4, which studies the early church's wrestling with its concepts of the Spirit and how Thomas Aquinas, John Calvin, and Friedrich Schleiermacher—who exemplify the Catholic, Reformed and Liberal theological traditions—came to terms with these issues.

After almost two centuries of reflections, certain questions remain unresolved. How independent is the Spirit? Is he simply the servant of Christ or the church or does he have freedom to create a world of his own? What is the Spirit's relation to the church? The New Testament suggests in some places that the Spirit is only given to the Christian community, in others it implies that the Spirit is present everywhere. What is at issue in each position? What are the implications of the various alternative ways of relating Spirit and church? What place should the experience of the Spirit occupy in Christianity? Some Christians have found the experience too dangerous and have practically banished it. Others have consigned the

Spirit to only a supporting role in Christian life. Some Spirit-filled groups insist the Spirit should occupy the center stage. Disagreements over the Spirit's role have almost fatally weakened the church in the present. Can these conflicts be resolved, and will such a resolution strengthen the church? Several options on all these questions are analyzed in the last chapter. A theology based on the Spirit in community, arising out of the present charismatic movement, provides needed insight into many of these issues and in doing so may prove itself the truly ecumenical theology of the future.

As a book about the Spirit in the modern world, this writing intends to raise more questions than it answers. New directions are sketched out, definite plans are eschewed. The future form of the church and its theology are left hazy, permanent organizations are forbidden. Some may find parts of this theology heavy, but the book itself intends to travel light and so be ready to follow the Spirit wherever he leads. Areas that appear basic to the work of the Spirit today—community, social responsibility, theological understanding—are analyzed as clearly as possible. But the theologian is not necessarily the prophet (and St. Paul implies that gifts of prophecy rank higher than theology), and so much remains sketchy. This is a prologue: It indicates places that need work and provides some of the tools necessary to the task. It does not, however, complete the job. That is up to the reader.

1
The Paradox of Community

The coming of the Holy Spirit was an explosion in the midst of the disciples. An incandescent burst, it lit up the image of Jesus. Before they had discussed him only in secret, now they could speak of nothing else on the streets of Jerusalem. When told that they must be silent or die, the disciples found the image of Christ so etched upon their minds that they preferred to face death rather than to erase it. A vehement blow, the exploding Spirit sent a tremor through them. The hesitant Peter now spoke with the authority Jesus had commanded; the disciples performed his miracles of healing. And even greater signs than Jesus had shown were seen as, it is said, about three thousand were converted in one day. A spiral of love, the Spirit's embrace drew them closer to one another. Throughout the book of Acts it is reported that the communal life of the first Christians was what attracted many to their assemblies.

SPIRIT AND COMMUNITY

The explosion of the Spirit did not scatter the disciples; rather, it pulled them together. Communal life was nothing new in the ancient world. Secret fraternities abounded in the Hellenistic age. Judaism itself gave rise to one of the most intense communities—a group of monks living by the Dead Sea in ascetic isolation. Long before, when Israel had come out of Egypt, the sons of Abraham said that God called them as a people with a common task and a common destiny. The early Christians were not a Hellenistic mystery cult. They proclaimed in the city squares the secret of their faith and subjected it to public debate. Nor were they a congregation of Essenes, hidden from the world in caves. Like the old, the new Israel was a body of people called together into community.

St. Paul, the greatest of the early Christian thinkers, was in large part a theologian of community. He prayed that his words would result in the formation of communities of Christians. He was not content to leave a place only having preached. He stayed until he had established a common life on a solid basis. He wrote back to his converts letters filled with directions and admonitions on living together. Most important, he saw that God's plan was not primarily to teach men new thoughts or even to redeem individuals from their sins but to transform creation into community.

In the letter to the Ephesians, Paul says:

> Grace was given to each of us according to the measure of Christ's gift. Therefore it is said "when he ascended on high he led the capturers into captivity and he gave gifts to men". . . . He ascended far above all the heavens that he might fill all things. And his gifts were

that some should be apostles, some prophets, some evangelists, some pastors and teachers for the uniting together of the saints to carry out the works of service and to build up the body of Christ. (Eph. 4:7-12)

In the same letter he wrote that the plan of God is to "unite together all things in heaven and on earth under the headship of Christ" (Eph. 1:4-10). Paul told the Colossians that the universe was created in order to be brought together under Christ (Col. 1:15-20). As Christ was the head of his body, the church, so someday he would be head of the whole cosmos.

Christ's ascension and the giving of the Spirit reveal, Paul says, that God's plan has a wider scope than just the salvation of men. "He ascended that he might fill all things." God's plan embraces all of creation. His object is to form the universe into a community in Christ. How is this plan carried out? Paul says that one way is through giving "gifts" to men. The gifts he mentions are all gifts for building up the church. Paul had told the church at Corinth:

To each is given a manifestation of the Spirit for the common good. To one the Spirit gives a word of wisdom, to another he gives a word of knowledge, to another faith, to another the gift of healing, to another the working of miracles, to another prophecy, to another various kinds of languages, to another the translations of these languages. . . . God has appointed in his church apostles, prophets, teachers, miracle workers, healers, helpers, administrators, speakers in various languages (1 Cor. 12:7-11).

Paul's argument is that God forms creation into community by filling it with his Spirit through these various gifts.

How do these rather ordinary-sounding (teachers, administrators, etc.) or, rather, bizarre-sounding (miracle workers, speakers in strange languages) spiritual gifts aid in God's plan to fill all creation with his presence? Paul's answer is that they serve to create community. Paul's metaphor of the church as a body is always in conjunction with his discussion of spiritual gifts (e.g., 1 Cor. 12). He writes to the Corinthians that each is given a manifestation of the Spirit *for the common good*. In Ephesians the Spirit is described in terms of the various offices in the church and the work of the Spirit is called completely joining together all the saints (*katartizo* means to unify and not to perfect as in the AV) in order to serve and to build up the Body of Christ (Eph. 4:12). According to the Apostle, the Spirit is given, in the first place, for the sake of the Body (e.g., 1 Cor. 12:7, 13, 27–28; 14:12). The Spirit basically belongs to the community. The Spirit is not, according to Paul, given primarily to individuals and is given to the church only to the extent that church is a collection of individuals with the Spirit. The Spirit is given primarily to the community and to individuals only to the extent that they participate in the community of the Spirit. The Church is not, for Paul, merely a collection of individuals; it is a body "fitly framed together" (Eph. 4:13–16).

Paul's emphasis is on the community rather than the individual, because of the connection between the Spirit, the community, and the plan of God. His argument is straightforward. The plan of God is the unification of all things under Christ. This is accomplished through filling all things with his presence. This filling of all things is, in turn, accomplished by the Ascension and the coming of the Spirit. Christ ascended that he might both fill all things and give men gifts to be used for building the church. The coming of the Spirit and the giving of spiritual gifts represents the beginning of God's plan to build creation into community. Filling the church with the Spirit and forming the church into community through the spiritual gifts represent another step toward the time when all things will be filled with the Spirit. The gifts of the Spirit and the subsequent Spirit-filled community are integral parts of God's plan. It is through them that God's plan to unify all things with his presence is carried out.

When the Spirit was poured on the disciples, that band became a Spirit-filled organism. As more were added to this body, the plan of God was carried forward. The Spirit-formed community is thus both an instrument of the plan of God and a sign of its progress. Through the enlargement of the community of the Spirit, more of God's creation is, in turn, filled with the Spirit. Paul also speaks of the work of the Spirit as a foretaste of the time when all creation will be a Spirit-filled community (Eph. 1:13-14; 2 Cor. 5:5). The church, Paul says, serves as an example of what life in community is like and gives us a taste of that time when all creation will be the Body of Christ.

Community, Paul implies, is the basis of Christian living. How does Paul understand this life? *Koinonia* (translated "community") is the common Greek word for the most intimate human relationships, including sexual union. Not only Paul, but most of the epistles, describe Christianity in terms of koinonia. To be a Christian is to be in community, to have koinonia. In Romans, Paul says the gentiles have come into a koinonia with the work of the Spirit (Rom. 15:27). In 1 Cor., he says men are called into koinonia with the Lord (1 Cor. 1:9). 1 John carries this theme further when it says "what we have seen and heard, we proclaim to you, so that you might have koinonia with us, our koinonia is with the Father and with his Son, Jesus Christ" (1 John 1:5). The two Petrine letters speak in the same way. 1 Peter says Christians share a koinonia with the Glory of God; 2 Peter says that men are promised koinonia with the divine nature (1 Pet. 5:1; 2 Pet. 1:4). These epistles, then, with remarkable consistency, describe the Christian experience of God in terms of this most intimate word. In Christ, mankind is brought into community with God.

Koinonia is also used to describe the Christian's relations with one another. Acts reports that the early converts gave themselves wholeheartedly to the Apostle's teachings, the breaking of bread, and the koinonia (Acts 2:42). Paul often speaks of his fellow Christians as those with whom he shares koinonia (Phil. 1:5; 2 Cor. 8:33). Paul implies that the Christian religion is an experience of intimate community with God and with one's fellow Christians. This is the standard by which he judges the experiences of his churches: does their religious experience produce an intimate relationship with Christ and an ever closer community among his people. Through the Spirit, Christians partake in the very life of God. This common life with God can only be lived out in a common life with those who share this Spirit. The koinonia of the Spirit, which Paul mentions to the Corinthians, is both koinonia with the Spirit and koinonia with fellow Christians created by the Spirit (2 Cor. 13:13).

The Spirit that fell on the early disciples created a community. Paul took this fact of early church history and gave it a theological interpretation. He forged a definition of the plan of God that encompassed not only the Creation, the history of Israel, the event of Christ, but also the coming of the Spirit and the foundation of the church. Starting with these later events, Paul saw the plan of God as the unification of all of creation under Christ and through the Spirit. Creation, Israel, Jesus, the church, all pointed toward this final community. Jesus was revealed as the head of this organism, and the salvation he obtained for mankind made it possible for them to share in a new communal life. The Spirit, with his gifts, created a community among those who shared in the new life made possible by the coming of Christ. This community, formed by the gifts of the Spirit, was to be an instrument and an example, pointing toward that time when he would unify all things.

At the close of the Apostolic age, community dropped out of the theological vocabulary. Although many of the early Christian writers were preoccupied with problems of ecclesiastical organization, they spent no time discussing the importance of koinonia. Nor do the fathers of the church use community as a basic theological term. Augustine wrote twenty-two books in his major work describing the City of God but in none of these does he suggest that the City of God will be a community of brothers and sisters. As the period of the church fathers turned into the middle ages, the organizational aspects of the church took precedence over its life as a community. Given the challenges the developing church faced from conflicting groups within her ranks and from hostile forces outside her congregations, this shift of emphasis from communal life to organizational structure was probably inevitable. The tightening of ecclesiastical forms allowed the church to survive the disputes of heretical groups, the crumbling of the Roman political order, and the invasion of barbarian warriors—and to preserve much of the greatness of Greek and Roman antiquity as well as of the Gospel. Organizational survival came at the cost of the experience of the church as community. The exception was the monastery. Though not ascetic, like the Essenes, the early Christian communities had been centers of strict morality in a licentious environment. While congregations were small and made up mostly of the lower classes, who had little of the world's goods to give up, it was easy for Christianity to maintain a life of simplicity and sacrifice. As the church grew and took on responsibility for large numbers and for different kinds of people, certain modifications in the rigorist ideal of the first century were necessary. Many, particularly in North Africa and Asia Minor, protested these new directions. Protest proved ineffective, but in Egypt a solution appeared: withdrawal from the congregations, but not the church, into isolated hermitages and small fraternities, where the ascetic ideal could be practiced unimpaired. Throughout the fourth and fifth centuries, as the political and economic situation deteriorated and the church became more adapted to the world, monasticism increased. Rules of life and forms of organization were drawn up for these communities. Many of the great leaders and theologians of the church came out of the monasteries. At the beginning of the middle ages, in the tenth and eleventh centuries, monasticism led a wave of reform that swept the church. During the medieval period, the monastery continued as a core of learning, spirituality, and renewal for the church.

Being celibate, the monastic communities were understood in terms of the dualistic morality of the middle ages. There were two orders of Christian life—the laity and the religious. Laymen lived in the world and the temptations and responsibilities of secular life kept their Christian lives from perfection. The religious, shielded from such temptations by vows of celibacy and poverty, could follow the ascetic ideal. Such vows were symbolic of the special grace needed to live the religious life. The ideal of community life was preserved by the monasteries but at the price of putting it beyond the reach of ordinary Christians. Life in a community required a special grace not open to those who lived in the world.

The most powerful challenge to this denial of Christian community came out of the left wing of the Reformation during the sixteenth century. In the twelfth century, the Waldensians had attempted to return the ideals of simplicity and community to ordinary Christians, and in the fourteenth century the Brethren of the Common Life fashioned small circles of shared mysticism. In the course of the sixteenth century, many were inspired by the reformers to carry the Reformation beyond Luther and Calvin. The reformers sought to purify the church of elements that could not be supported by Scripture. The Anabaptists wanted to roll back the intervening centuries and restore the Christianity of the first century. They demanded that the church be broken up into congregations living the New Testament pattern of strict morality and communal life. When the church responded to this demand by persecution, they withdrew from the church into small clusters, where they lived lives of exemplary simplicity and service. Even their enemies confessed they were models of Christian living. Such high perfection came at a high cost. As aware as any medieval monk of the temptations of worldly responsibility, the Anabaptists secluded themselves from the world and renounced any responsibility for the society.

Behind the appeal for stricter standards was the perception of the world as evil. Only those who rejected the societies of men and sheltered themselves in the community of saints could live pure Christian lives. The church was to be "an island of holiness in the sea of sin" as one Anabaptist writer put it. The Anabaptists restored the ideal of Christian community, but they made it synonymous with sectarian withdrawal from the world. To live in community was to abandon the world.

THE COMMUNAL IDEAL IN AMERICA

The communal ideal went underground in Europe with the persecution of the Anabaptists. In the next century it was transported across the sea to the new world, where it found a permanent home.[1] The Puritans, who carved a settlement log by log and boulder by boulder out of the wilderness that was New England, came to establish a heavenly Kingdom upon the earth. Their preachers spoke of it as a "city set upon a hill," a society so divinely ordered that the nations of the earth would be captivated by it and reform themselves along its lines. The major architect of their political order, John Winthrop, described the New England colony as a "model of Christian charity." What is striking about Winthrop's description of the colony is that he applies all of St. Paul's metaphors for the church to colonial society. In Winthrop's eyes New England was to be "the Body of Christ," a unified organism animated by love, where every member served the common good rather than his own private advantage. Massachusetts Bay was to be a commonwealth, a title it carries to this day, where everyone cooperated with each other to extend the well-being of the community and the work of God's providence rather than the pursuit of selfish riches. Colonial Massachusetts was America's first religious commune and it embedded this vision, as it did so many things, into the heart of the developing nation.

For awhile it appeared that the developing nation would develop in an antireligious direction. After the Revolutionary War, the influence of French culture, and therefore French skepticism, increased in the new country through its alliance with France. Its leaders were skeptics like Jefferson and Franklin or religious liberals like Washington and Adams. But no sooner had the nation settled down to business when the breath of the Spirit again blew on the land. From the roughhewn frontiers of Kentucky and Tennessee to the sedate countryside of New England, men and women were falling into fits of salvation in what historians term the second great awakening. The frontier rolled out into western New York bringing the revival with it, until the area west of the Allegheny mountains became known as the "burned-over district"—so often had it been burned over by the fires of religious revival. Out of this tidal surge of enthusiasm, with its belief that God's Spirit was working with a radically new presence and power, came a sense that the end of the world was soon to come. "Hadn't the pouring out of the Spirit been prophecied as a sign of the end since the prophet Joel?" many asked. And if God's Spirit was truly present in people in a new way, and if it was really the presence of a Holy Spirit, the conclusion was obvious—men and women possessed of this Spirit were holy, too. The union of these two beliefs—the imminent coming of the Kingdom and the perfection of the redeemed—produced new forms of religious community.

Ann Lee arrived in America before the Revolution and moved to upstate New York before it was burned over. She and her family were members of a schismatic group of Quakers in England. The Quakers were born of a wave of religious enthusiasm that had swept England a century earlier and they had not been sneeringly called Quakers for nothing—it was said that they trembled and quaked when the Spirit came upon them. In the course of the eighteenth century in England and America the quaking died down and the Society of Friends (as they came to be called) achieved a counting-house respectability around London and Philadelphia. Disturbed by the cessation of quaking and other signs of religious fervor among the Friends, a group broke off from them in the middle of the eighteenth century and began to manifest again the more frenzied signs of the Spirit. They shook and trembled, they danced and sang, and they were derisively labeled shaking Quakers or just plain Shakers. Jailed, beaten, and stoned (as were the Quakers before them), a group of Shakers led by Ann Lee fled to America and settled in New York in 1774.

Mother Ann Lee was said to be at least a prophet, if not the female incarnation of Christ. She believed that at conversion one enters a state of heavenly perfection and, since it is written in the Bible that in heaven "they neither marry or are given in marriage," her followers were celibate. They lived in communities, worked the soil, and made beautiful handicrafts which have now become valuable antiques. Their meetings were scenes of controlled enthusiasm where they danced complex dances accompanied by elaborate hymns of their own composing. During the second great awakening they sent out teams of missionaries and established "families" (as they called their communities) throughout the new nation. Despite their celibacy their community life was not monastic or even ascetic. Their overflowing energy, boundless joy, and practical sense made them the model for others who would take up communal experiments. They demonstrated that religious communes could be successful and orderly and thus survive, as theirs would for over a century. Religious leaders came to visit and learn, and secular utopianists like Robert Owen studied their societies.

The ideas of heavenly perfection on earth and the imminent return of Christ became part of the American evangelical mind in the first decades of the nineteenth century. Those who combined fervent piety and pragmatic sense, like the Shakers, made these ideas into flourishing communities. These qualities were epitomized by John Humphrey Noyes. Converted during the revival, Noyes received a vision in 1833 telling him that Christ had, in fact, already come. The second coming had taken place in A.D. 70 and now those who were saved were already in heaven. Noyes took this to mean that believers could not sin no matter what they did. Thus sexual relations among the redeemed were not carnal but spiritual and therefore, as Noyes wrote, "In a holy community, there is no more reason why sexual intercourse should be restrained by law, than why eating and drinking should be." He called his system of unrestrained sexuality "complex marriage" and, when combined with a form of birth control, it became the basis of his perfectionist community, where the redeemed could live on earth as they would in heaven.

He began his community in Putney, Vermont, but, to the Yankee mind, sex was sex and Noyes's idea of complex marriage landed him in jail on charges of adultery. He jumped bail and moved his followers to Oneida, New York—the heart of the burned-over district, which was more tolerant of religious experimentation and near the Canadian border, in case further retreat was called for. Beginning as a farm, the Oneida community soon branched out into prosperous manufacturing. The community burgeoned, with its rare combination of revivalist perfectionism and American industry. The second generation, however, inherited only the founders' business sense. Some were agnostics and few experienced the power of the Spirit's sanctifying fire. Oneida survived the attacks of outsiders and the accusations of immorality but was fatally weakened by the internal dissension of the younger generation, who could not share the religion of their fathers. In 1881, the system of complex marriage was stopped and the community became a stock company, which carried on the vast enterprises. Although it did not last as long as the Shaker society, Oneida, too, demonstrated to America that a pouring out of the Spirit might result in communal living and that a religious vision of a more perfect society could be translated into a stable community on earth.

To the west of Oneida, a few years before Noyes arrived in New York, another son of the burned-over district, Joseph Smith, was praying in the woods. Suddenly two angels revealed to him the location of plates of gold that told how the American Indians were the lost tribes of Israel, and that America was to be the site of the second coming. Published in 1830 as *The Book of Mormon*, Smith's revelations became the basis of a community of converts who held all goods in common and practiced polygamy. Popular hatred of their communal living and sexual practices forced them further and further west. Each time they thought they were settled, area residents gathered into mobs and drove them further along the frontier. Mormon practices earned Smith and his brother a lynching in

Illinois, and under the command of Brigham Young the community fled to the far west and the banks of the great Salt Lake, where they could practice their communal life in peace. Like the Shakers and the Oneida community, the Mormons illustrate a peculiarly American blend of intense emotional piety, religious community, unusual sexual practices, and extremely successful business enterprises.

Vast changes took place in the society after the Civil War, which seemed to mark the end of American communal experiments. A continuing demographic shift from the farms to the cities began, mirroring an economic trend from agriculture to industry. Rural life was rejected in favor of the excitements of the city. The Shakers and those ancient religious communities, the monasteries, survived, and the transplanted descendants of the sixteenth-century Anabaptists, the Mennonites, the Amish, and various German Brethren groups, continued to live in agricultural isolation from the mainstream of America. In general, the age of the commune seemed over with the decline of the rural ethos and the evaporation of the wild perfectionistic religion of Mother Ann Lee and the burned-over district. The Mormons, in exchange for statehood, gave up their polygamous deviation from sexual norms and their communism and settled down to life as a respectable denomination.

PENTECOSTAL COMMUNALISM

At the beginning of the twentieth century, when the impetus for community seemed to have dried up in American society, particularly in American Christianity, and a new search for community on the part of the young was over half a century away, a spiritual underground began in American religion, which would, in time, create another thrust for community. St. Paul said that the Spirit formed community through certain gifts like teaching and prophecy and working miracles. Although Paul's emphasis on community continued in a truncated form throughout much of Christian history, his stress on these spiritual gifts died out in the first few centuries. The rediscovery of these spiritual gifts, particularly the ones that appear most extraordinary, launched the underground movement known as Pentecostalism, at the turn of the century.

Pentecostalism began quite spontaneously when a group of evangelical Protestants began meeting in an old Bible School in Kansas to try to recapture the power of the apostles in the book of Acts. Suddenly and unexpectedly, they began to experience what they took to be modern counterparts of the gifts Paul enumerates in his letters. They spoke in unknown languages, they performed miracles. At first they did not realize what was happening, but after reading the New Testament they correlated their experiences with Paul's descriptions and became convinced that they had rediscovered something that had been lost in the course of Christian history. Out of this experience came the basic claim of the Pentecostal movement, that Christians today can experience the same gifts of the Spirit that the first Christians did.[2]

Members of this group began to describe their experiences to their Protestant brethren. They were rejected on all fronts, driven from their churches, and forced to start their own, Pentecostal, denominations. Six years after the first outbreak in Kansas, a black Pentecostal evangelist began meetings in Los Angeles. Thousands were attracted, and from there the movement spread throughout the world. For most of the twentieth century, Pentecostalism remained underground. Neither the mainline Protestant churches nor the evangelical denominations wanted anything to do with it. Most Americans were not aware of its existence.

The early Pentecostal converts and leaders came from American evangelical Protestantism. American evangelicalism had lost its pre-Civil War communitarian ethos and had opted for bourgeois individualism, along with the rest of American society. Since this was their heritage, the new Pentecostal experience did not lead to a new drive for community. Rather they interpreted their experience of the Spirit in the terms of evangelical theology. They called this experience the "baptism in the Holy Spirit" and they understood it by analogy with the evangelical idea of conversion as a private experience in each person's life.

The early Pentecostals regained Paul's own emphasis on the spiritual gifts, but, due to their inheritance from American evangelicalism, they did not see the gifts in the same way as Paul did. Rather than emphasize the communal nature of the spiritual gifts, the Pentecostals implied that these gifts belonged primarily to the individual and not to the Body. Rather than concentrate on the place of the Spirit in the universal plan of God, they focused almost exclusively on individual salvation. These carry-overs from the ethos of American pietism kept the Pentecostals from realizing the corporate and cosmic dimensions of the work of the Spirit.

The Pentecostal movement did not stay underground forever. Fifty years after its beginnings in Kansas, it had infiltrated most of the major denominations, and the Pentecostal churches were gaining publicity as the fastest-growing religious bodies in the world. In the early 1950s, a

Pentecostal leader, David du Plessis, came to New York to explain the Pentecostal movement to executives of the World Council of Churches, and after those meetings he was invited continually to major Protestant churches, universities, and seminaries to discuss the movement. Throughout the fifties, small groups of clergy and lay people in the mainline denominations met to learn about and experience the gifts of the Spirit. Few of these groups knew of each other's existence; few outside of them had any idea what was happening. Then, in 1960, Father Dennis Bennett of Van Nuys, California, who had been involved in one of these groups and found that the growth of this experience within his Episcopal congregation was creating rumors, publicly acknowledged his charismatic activity. A storm of controversy followed: an assistant minister stormed from the church, Father Bennett's resignation was requested and received, his Bishop issued a letter banning charismatic meetings. Newspapers picked up the story; wire services spread it across the country; *Time* and *Newsweek* carried articles on "speaking in tongues." The glare of publicity brought these groups to light; charismatic pastors and laymen in every denomination were suddenly exposed to suspicion and sometimes harassment. Still the movement spread.

People from almost every Protestant church continued to seek and receive the experience of spiritual gifts. In the early sixties charismatic groups appeared at major universities and seminaries around the country. Gradually other clergymen beside Father Bennett began to publicly discuss charismatic spirituality: Lutheran Pastor, Larry Christenson, wrote several articles on this experience for Lutheran audiences; the Reverend James Brown, a Presbyterian, spoke throughout his denomination, explaining spiritual gifts; Reverend Harold Bredesen, a Reformed Church pastor, traveled around the nation introducing various congregations to this movement. A decade later, in the seventies, these efforts swelled into large organizations in many Protestant denominations: Lutherans, Presbyterians, and Episcopalians have national charismatic committees, which publish newsletters, arrange conferences, and work to keep the movement in the mainstream of their denomination. In 1974, the Lutherans held such a conference in Minnesota, which attracted several thousand people.

In 1967 a group of Roman Catholics from Duquesne University unexpectedly began to experience the same things. From Duquesne the movement spread to Notre Dame University. A small group from Notre Dame moved to Ann Arbor, Michigan, to work with university students. In a year a meeting that began with 10 students had grown to 125, and in three years to 500. There are now almost 1,000 people committed to the charismatic community in Ann Arbor. They come together at least once a week for a large prayer meeting and many have broken down into smaller households where six or eight people live together. The community runs various classes for its members, to teach them about life in community. Members are encouraged to live in some form of household where families take in single people, or to share a house, or where students live together. Most are engaged in some service, whether publishing a monthly magazine of the charismatic movement, visiting in the local hospitals, or ministering to the college students.

These Catholics experienced the same things as the Pentecostals, but they did not have the same evangelical background and so they understood the experience differently. Given the importance of the church in Catholic theology, they saw the spiritual gifts in terms of their place in the Body of Christ and spoke of the gifts in ways closer to those of the Apostle Paul—as being for the common good and the building up of the Body. The practical result of this understanding was that their experience of the Spirit led immediately to a new concern for Christian community. The charismatic students and faculty of Notre Dame and Ann Arbor sought out ways to grow closer together. Some moved into communal houses; others sought to meet in a regular and disciplined way. They looked for ways to teach and to serve each other. From Ann Arbor and Notre Dame this model of Christian community has spread with the catholic charismatic movement around the world.

MODERN COMMUNES

At the same time the churches were discovering the charismatic movement and the charismatic movement was discovering the importance of community, young people suddenly but unobtrusively began packing their suitcases, leaving their suburban homes, and moving back onto the farms and into the woods in small clusters of humanity. In the late sixties they appeared on almost every major highway: adolescents with kinky hair running down their backs, knapsacks on their shoulders, guitars in hand, hitchhiking to Utopia, going out, as one of their songs says, "to look for America." Propelled by the same vision that landed the Puritans on the rocky coasts of New England, driven by the same feelings that urged the pioneers over the mountains and onto the western plains, they left behind the old world with its schedules and its tapestry of insoluble problems and sought a new world of freedom and happiness. Disillusionment with technological society, which promised paradise and delivered polluted waters, slums, and people programmed onto computer cards, spawned hundreds of groups who sought in communal living a more humane style of life.[3]

Instead of burning down the society, these communards established an alternative to it. Some who had dropped out of the mainstream dropped back into smaller societies of their own making. As the sixties turned into the seventies, professional people, physicians, lawyers, professors, began to pool themselves and their training into law communes, communal medical centers, and alternative schools where students and faculty lived together. It was not a unified movement. Some moved in together because it made life cheaper and easier. Some grew together out of intensely personal but shared experiences of religious vision, artistic creation, or political action. Some came together out of a deep compulsion to experiment. "It was a spontaneous movement . . . only afterwards was it called a movement. At the outset, it was the gut reaction of a generation," writes commune chronicler Robert Houriet, who estimates that over two thousand such communes sprang up in the last half of the 1960s.[4] These eddies of human collectivity swirled into being spontaneously. Drawn together by the currents of the age, they were only dimly aware of each other.

Few secular communards even glanced at Christianity. Although monastaries and convents flourished, their ideal of life in community made no impact on the average Catholic parish. Koinonia remained reserved for those under special vows, and the Catholic church went ahead building up massive congregations of thousands of souls, with little attempt to form the laity into any community beyond that provided by neighborhood or ethnic identification. The revivalistic piety, which had nurtured the Shaker families, the Oneida community, and the Mormon's communism, was harnessed, after the Civil War, to the developing ethos of individualism in the golden age of the robber barons, Horatio Alger, and the myth of the self-made man. Protestants ceased to see the church as the communal Body of Christ and regarded it as a collection of individuals who happened to share the same religious experience. Amish and Mennonites became tourist attractions for suburban church members. Moving out of their families, the communards often left behind dense urban parishes and piecemeal suburban congregations.

Hastily painted Victorian houses sprang up in the cities and roughhewn farms and log cabins were cut from the wilderness and seen by the communards as alternatives to the high-rise apartment and the split-level house. How much of an alternative were they? The frequency with which the communes of the sixties seemed to disband and regroup reflects more the transience of American society than a constructive alternative. In the large apartment complex where we once lived, moving vans made almost daily visitations, and the bank from which I got my home mortgage figures that the average American family lives in a house for no more than five years. The communal counterpart of the moving van, the overstuffed backpack, apparently appeared as frequently at their doors as moving vans in a new housing development. The "do your own thing" mentality, which slowly paralyzed and strangled many early communes, represents no radical break. It is only a replay of the laissez-faire individualism in American culture, which spawned the system the communards sought to escape. Writes Houriet:

> Everywhere hassles and marathon encounter meetings that couldn't resolve questions like whether to leave the dogs in or out. Everywhere, cars that wouldn't run and pumps that wouldn't pump because everyone knew all about the occult history of tarot and nobody knew anything about mechanics. Everywhere, people who strove for self-sufficiency and freedom from the capitalist system but accepted food stamps and handouts from Daddy, a corporate sales V.P. Sinks filled with dishes, cows wandering through gates left open, and no one to blame. Everywhere, instability, transiency. Somebody was always splitting, rolling up his bag, packing his guitar and kissing good-bye—off again in search of the truly free, unhungup community.[5]

Accounts sympathetic to these communal attempts report that their problems were more the problems of the old system than of a new one. The communes reflected more than they avoided the pitfalls of the culture they sought to escape.[6]

Before one can seek an alternative to one's society one must, at least partially, stand outside the society. One who is totally immersed and shaped by one's culture has no platform from which to criticize it. Only one who can back off from his society and have some perspective on it can evaluate its strengths and weaknesses and be free enough from it to form alternatives. One might call this stance of standing back from one's society the transcendence of society. For some young people this transcendence was the result of reading social critics like Marx or C. Wright Mills or Herbert Marcuse, who gave them a new perspective on their society and enabled them to view it from some intellectual distance. For others, the experience of visiting wholly different countries, particularly through the Peace Corps, gave them a new set of eyes through which to see their native land. Those who worked with illiterate children in the Philippines, or starving children in Africa, came back with new perspectives on America's waste and consumption. Thus, in the course of the sixties, many young people found themselves in a state of transcendence, or, as they called it, "alienation," from their society. Some just dropped into the pit of alienation and were swallowed up by it, others sought alternatives in communal living.

But their perspectives on society were almost wholly negative. They knew clearly what they were running from but not as clearly what they were running toward. Their criticisms of society were clear and concrete, honed to a sharp point by the analytic precision of Marx, Mills, and Marcuse, and backed with the evidence of a vast army of new experiences gained from LSD and marathon encounter groups. Their alternatives, on the other hand, were phrased in the vaguest of generalities and platitudes about a more "human" style of life or the value of "freedom" and "experience." Many of the communards didn't seem to grasp the way in which problems are interrelated, and thus their transcendence of their society was lopsided. They knew what they wanted to reject and what problems they wanted to avoid, but they didn't know these problems were a part of the total fabric of American life, of which they, too, were a part. Thus they brought the same problems into their communes.

The problems now came dressed in long hair and beads

rather than in suits and ties, but they were still the basic problems of American society. Seeking a stability denied them in the world of suburbia, they created communes that disbanded as frequently as suburban households. Rejecting the nuclear family, they scorned legal marriage and simply moved in together in couples and in communal marriages, only to be plagued by the same interpersonal problems that they saw in their parents and peers. Rejecting technological society, they still found themselves addicted to a type of music that demanded the most sophisticated electronic wizardry to produce or to listen to. Some came with stereos and amplified guitars, which they couldn't maintain or repair for lack of the most elementary knowledge of electronics. Seeking to escape the confines of empirical reality they delved into the occult, only to find that magic was no substitute for machinery when it came to pumping water or getting the crops to market. And so, rather than overcoming the polarization in our society between the sciences and the humanities, between technical mastery and human wisdom, they exacerbated the split.

THE NATURE OF COMMUNITY

Community is by definition the transcendence of self. To live in community (whether it is an affair, a marriage, a family, a commune, a church, or a society) is to get enough distance from one's own needs, wants, desires, and preoccupations, so that one can share in those of others as well as one's own. It is to have enough grasp on oneself, so that one can accommodate oneself to the patterns others set, as well as trying to accommodate others to oneself. The fact that community means the negation of selfness (a major motif in all religions) may provide a clue as to why, in general, religious communities have grown strong and abiding. Part of the religious experience seems to be stripping away part of the armor-plate of self-regard, and this is the first step in building community. Jesus said, "He who loses his life shall find it." This must have been one of the first principles of the early Christian communities. One must lose the old life of self in order to gain a new life in community.

This may also provide some clue as to why so many of the communes founded in the 1960s got into trouble. Although many were founded on a positive vision of what a new life might be, many were also founded out of negation, as a reaction against what life had been. In reaction against the asserted "dehumanization" of life by technical society, communes were seen by many as centers of human support. In reaction against the asserted exploitiveness of industrial society, communes were seen as places where people could "realize themselves." In reaction against the asserted materialism of the modern era, communes were seen as retreats where "spiritual potential" could be developed. They were conceived as asylums for refugees from the psychic warfare of the larger society. They were conceived of as treatment centers for the broken and bloodied soul of modern man. The literature of communes is full of such phrases as "getting oneself together," "searching for wholeness," "realizing one's true self." In other words, many communes were founded for "therapeutic" reasons.[7]

A "therapeutic" (to borrow Philip Rieff's term) commune is one gathered primarily to fill some "human need." The therapeutic mentality sees people (and especially oneself) as a conglomeration of "needs" that must be satisfied. The raison d'être of the therapeutic commune is to "get oneself together," fulfill one's potential, enrich or enlarge one's psychic life. One therefore joins a commune in the hope that certain therapeutic benefits will be reaped—problems will be "worked through," potential (creative, spiritual, sexual, or whatever) will be fulfilled, consciousness will be expanded. The focus of such commune members is wholly on themselves. Their primary commitment is to their own psychological well-being. First and foremost, they seek satisfaction of their "human needs." The community becomes not the transcendence of self but another means to further absorption into the needs of oneself. Even in those communes based on the techniques of "group" psychology, the group is seen primarily as a means to one's own therapy or self-realization. One is concerned about the needs of others, if at all, only in the insidious hope that this policy will aid in meeting one's own needs.

Communal gatherings of those driven by therapeutic motivation might be pictured as a circle of empty vessels, each waiting to be filled. Since every vessel is empty, no one has anything to pour into the gaping containers. At best, there can only be a sharing of problems. That is the one commodity not in short supply. Such gatherings can be counterproductive if the participants become disillusioned and embittered and driven further within themselves. The paradox of the therapeutically motivated commune is well summarized by a discouraged commune leader whom Houriet interviewed. "American society must produce neurotic individuals and this is no less true of its rebels than of its reformers," he replied to Houriet. "It is said that happy people don't volunteer to go to war. Neither, I say, do they join communes."[8] If communes are based primarily on serving individual needs, then the "happy people" (presumably those whose needs are relatively well met by the process of their life) don't need communes. Although, presumably, they could function well within them. The unhappy people (those who seem empty) need the commune because of their emptiness but, precisely because of that emptiness, cannot make it work, for they appear to have little to give to it and are too focused in on themselves to get out of themselves enough to build community.

This dilemma is even more intense for those communes based explicitly on a therapeutic ideology. A group of students I met once might serve as a parable of this. Freshly back from an "encounter" weekend, they decided to put the principles they had gleaned to work by moving in together. All felt the need of further group experience as an aid in solving their individual problems. Soon one of two things began to happen to them. For some the treatment worked. They began to get over their problems. Thus they no longer needed the therapeutic community for therapy. The very effectiveness of the group presented them with an even more painful problem than those it had solved—to leave the group, since it was no longer "needed," and thus to abandon the community, or to stay with the community in ever-increasing frustration, since they no longer felt the need for the therapy that bound the group together. For others, for whom the group did not work or who could not face the pain of leaving, the community did not solve their problems but only rationalized them and confirmed them. Soon these people were saying that life with problems, life under the sign of perpetual therapy, was the only authentic way to live.

The question is not whether communes ought to meet human needs or even to be therapeutic. Clearly communes can and ought to support and improve human life. The question is whether those communes founded explicitly (or implicitly) for therapeutic reasons can really function therapeutically. Perhaps it is only those communities with visions larger than just the fulfillment of individual needs that can really fulfill human needs, for they not only supply salve for wounded psyches but also direct people beyond their bundles of needs to larger vistas. Communes founded primarily out of a sense of emptiness may never be able to fill that void. Communities that gather together those who need to have their needs fulfilled and their problems solved may never be able to accomplish that task. They may keep people fixated on their psyches and bar them from building community.

It is precisely because the fulfillment of man's basic needs is so important that it can't be left to those groups who specialize in it. Their premise is no doubt correct from the viewpoint of Christian theology—man is fulfilled only in community. But focusing only on man's need for community will not build community, for community is the transcendence of the needs of self, even the need for community. Perhaps only those communities that do not aim primarily at the fulfillment of human needs actually meet human needs. Those that concentrate on therapy fail in the first task of building community, the transcendence of self. This is part of the paradox of community; it is also part of the paradox of Christian faith. One must lose one's life in order to gain it. One must transcend one's own needs in order to have them met.

During the same decade that young people were taking to the woods in search of utopia the church, in the form of the charismatic movement, was rediscovering the experience of Spirit-filled koinonia. Those young people who spontaneously left home glimpsed a basic truth of the · Christian faith that had been lost in America since the triumph of individualism and was just being recovered by the Pentecostal movement: that human life is basically communal. The youngsters heading for utopia realized from the depths of their unanalyzed alienation that one must see a vision and even undergo the experience of a new world before one is free enough of the old world to erect an alternative to it. The early Christians were shaken loose from their culture by the mind-blowing experiences of the Resurrection of Jesus and the outpouring of the Spirit of God. These experiences created a community of loving fellowship and spiritual power that came to regard the wisdom of their society as the height of foolishness. Even though they could not always put it into practice, the modern seekers after utopia learned that man is meant to live in community and that, in a world of selfishness and individualism, the building of community must begin with the transcendence of culture. The churches could relearn these basic Christian truths from them.

INDIVIDUALS, COMMUNITIES, SOCIETY

The story of the search for utopia in the sixties and seventies illustrates the paradoxes of community: that the old society must be transcended before a new one can come into being; and that one must get beyond one's own needs before community can be built. In different terms, these two paradoxes are found in Christian teaching: The church must be in the world but not of it and he who would gain his life must lose it. The rising above one's culture and egocentricity, which must be the foundation of any new community, is what the Christian means by conversion. There are two reasons why there is an intimate connection between conversion and community. First, conversion, Paul says, means dying to oneself. Paul likens baptism to a kind of death (Rom. 6:3-4). Becoming a Christian means killing the introversion of the self into its own world and pushing it out of the circle of its own egotism. This liberates one from the old world as well as the old man. Breaking free from the past with its history of self-centeredness allows one to escape the influences of the society that helped mold one into a selfish form. Conversion is the theological name for that experience that is the foundation of community—the transcendence of self.

Second, conversion entails community, because the conversion experience can only be sustained in a converted community. Man is a social being and he must be supported and formed by some society. Social science and the sociology of knowledge have reinforced this presupposition of biblical experience. Simply changing an individual's beliefs or feelings about God, or his moral attitudes, and then having him formed and influenced by a society of skepticism and egotism, will not produce vital Christianity. Often conversion has been seen as simply a change of mind, after which one lives in a hostile society much as one did before. Without a community providing nourishment and support such a superficial faith sinks few roots and produces little fruit. Conversion, for St. Paul, was not only the transition from one state of mind to another but the transition from one community to another. Conversion meant leaving behind the "wisdom of the world," that society that supports selfishness and skepticism, and entering into the "wisdom of God," a society that sustains faith and service. Conversion led inevitably to community in the New Testament because conversion was a community-creating experience, and because this experience could only fully develop in a community that strengthened it.

The Anabaptists of the sixteenth century understood this all too well. Realizing for the first time that Christianity must create and be lived in community made them overly sensitive to the conflict between the wisdom of the world and the way of the community. Like the medieval monks, they felt the only way to maintain the faith was to withdraw from the world. Nowhere does the New Testament condone such sectarianism. Paul explicitly condemns it. Apparently Paul once wrote to the church at Corinth to disassociate themselves from immoral people (this may be the fragment of one of his letters that is preserved in 2 Cor. 6:14-7:1). Misunderstanding, the Corinthians believed him to mean they should not associate themselves with any non-Christian, but leave the world behind. Paul had to write them again, correcting this overly sectarian misunderstanding (cf. 1 Cor. 5:9-10) and exhorting them not to attempt to "go out of the world." In the same way, Jesus tells the disciples in John that they are to be "in the world but not of it." The Anabaptists, and sectarians throughout the ages, misconstrue an emphasis on community to mean not being of the world by being in the world as little as possible.

Actually, the Anabaptists had in their own experience the resource to enable them to be in the world without being of it and so avoid sectarianism. That resource was Christian community. Living in community provides the Christian the means to work in the world without being overcome.
The New Testament pictures Christians gathering in community but not hiding in it. From the assemblies they went out to earn their livings, to preach their gospel, and to oppose their enemies. Community was not a fortress, as it

often appears to be in the sectarian mentality, but a staging area from which one drew sustenance and power. The sixteenth-century Anabaptists understood that conversion must lead to community, but they made the assembled community into a barricaded sect.

Americans have generally individualized the idea of conversion too much. It is simply an event in the personality of the individual who, upon becoming a Christian, gains new emotions or understands new doctrines or assumes new moral attitudes. A full New Testament understanding of conversion is not a change in one's state of mind but the transition from one world to another, one community to another. Leaving behind the community of selfishness marked by sin and death, one acquires at least the foretaste of a new community of life and power. The individualizing of religion in America has blunted the radical thrust of Christian conversion. This facet of American religion is part of the culture of individualism, which must be overcome if Christian community is to form.

The impossibility of growing community in the soil of bourgeois individualism not only haunts the church in America; the same problem thwarts the creation of community in the therapeutic ethos of encounter groups and sensitivity sessions. Such experiences do much to free people from their past and give them a taste of deepened personal relations. But any therapeutic technique focuses primarily on the individual and his needs. People returning from such experiences usually talk most about how much better *they* feel and not much about how the experience affected anyone beside themselves. The therapeutic ethos drives the individual deeper into himself, into his own needs and feelings, and blocks the first step in the formation of community—the transcendence of self. The privatizing of experience in America—whether it is the conversion experience of the evangelical with "my" Jesus or the psychological experience of the therapeutic—defies the creation of community. In America only religious communities have survived any length of time. The Shakers began to die because of their celibacy, but the monasteries and Anabaptist settlements are the longest continuing communes in America. Socialist and utopian attempts folded in the course of the nineteenth century, long before Oneida became a corporation or the Mormons chose respectability over community. The most enthusiastic of all, the Shakers, were still holding on when the last of the other evangelical communes had dissipated. The transcendence of self is a basic theme in almost all religions and perhaps only religion provides a hefty enough dose of self-denial to solidify the foundations of community. Socialist ideology and therapeutic experience are potent forces, but perhaps only the Spirit's baptism by fire can melt the block of selfishness so firmly entrenched in the heart of every American by his country's myths of rugged individualism and self-made success.

In the sixties two things were happening to recall to American Christianity neglected aspects of her tradition: Communes sprang up, calling the churches out of their individualism to a new awareness of community; and charismatics appeared, awakening the church's sensitivity to the Spirit. Youngsters seeking to create community rediscovered for the church two neglected aspects of Christianity: that life ought to be communal and that community demands going beyond oneself (i.e., it demands conversion). Because of their lopsided transcendence of culture, which simply rejected aspects of America they didn't happen to like and the therapeutic ethos that underlay much communal experimentation, actual community remained paradoxical to the communal movement. The communards did not go beyond America as much as they simply criticized parts of it and thus took over many of its basic assumptions into their communities. These assumptions, which stressed self-fulfillment over service to others, self-assertion over cooperation, and "doing your own thing" over mutual responsibility, were antithetical to community and got them into trouble. All the world's religions testify that the experience of God creates sufficient self-denial to form community. From the standpoint of the Gospel, community remains a clear imperative. Only conversion, not ideology or therapy, can create the self-transcendence that generates community. The secular world will never produce abiding koinonia, for it cannot get out of itself enough to subject itself to thoroughgoing criticism or drive people out of their selfish dominance. Community will always remain paradoxical and illusive to the world. Only the church can unravel the paradoxes of community, for only the experience of the Spirit can shake men loose enough from themselves and their society to not only glimpse new worlds but to have the humility and the power to put them into practice.

CREATING COMMUNITY

Putting community into practice raises the final paradox of community—we cannot create community no matter how hard we try. Handbooks for building community have existed through the centuries, yet no lasting communities have been built by these techniques. Why? Because these books deal with matters of external structure, of getting organized: Small groups or large? Living in one place or only meeting together frequently? Sharing a common ideology or encouraging diversity? But community is not a matter of external structure. Koinonia is basically an experience, a style of living. Structures and organization are important but they are derived and not primary. They do not create community, they only express the koinonia if it's present. They must grow naturally out of the more basic experience of community. Concentrating on organization as a means to community will construct only a skeleton, not a living body.

Community is not dependent upon any single technique or structure. I have been a member of a charismatic community of 500 people, where the sense of koinonia astonished the most skeptical observers who visited us. I have visited groups of 10 or 12 living under the same roof, where there was only hostility and resentment. I know religious communities that include conservative businessmen and long-haired dropouts, nuns and former prostitutes. No common ideology or background binds them together, only the single experience of the Spirit. I have stayed in communes with all middle-class students of the same political beliefs who could hardly stand one another. Community is not primarily a function of the things organizational manuals deal with (structure, ideology, etc.). Of themselves, these will not create community. If the experience of community is present, it can manifest itself in any of a number of structures—in large groups of several hundred as well as small groups of ten or twelve, in groups that meet together only once or twice a week, as well as in households living under the same roof.

Many have neglected this fact that community must be experienced before it can be constructed. I knew a group of students, all deeply involved in the counterculture, who wanted to live communally. They bought a house and moved in together. Because they shared the common experience of dropping out and turning on, because they dressed alike and agreed on most points of political theory, they assumed they were a community. They soon found they weren't. Personal habits became annoying but there was no means or willingness to compromise. Lacking a process for decision making, problems basic to the survival of the group went unsolved. They could never resolve the dilemma of privacy versus openness within the group. When too many people "crashed" their place they couldn't agree on expelling them, until so many new people drifted in that the venture collapsed. A more tragic example involves groups of Roman Catholic nuns and priests. In the last few years the Catholic church has closed many large convents and monastic houses and allowed the members to live together in smaller houses and apartments. The strict rule and discipline in a convent allowed a multiplicity of people to coexist. Many naively felt this meant they were a community. When the rule and discipline were removed by allowing them to live communally in small settings, many discovered they just couldn't get along with their "sister" or "brother." In both cases many felt guilt about the failure of "community." They shouldn't have; koinonia is a gift of the Spirit, not a natural human possibility. In both cases they moved into community before they actually had a community.

 The paradox of the practice of community is that it cannot be practiced. The experience of koinonia is a gift. It is something given us, not something we create. Some people find they are open to the experience of community, some groups find they suddenly *are* a community and can begin to structure themselves accordingly. Since there are no techniques for building community and community is a gift of the Spirit, community may remain forever paradoxical to our society and maybe even to our churches. We are all interested in what we can do. In meetings in all the institutions of our society—church, academy, business—the same question is raised, "how can we organize?" "what can we do?" "what is the best technique?" This is the mark of Cain upon us, it is the sign of our overactivistic and technique-saturated culture upon our foreheads. I know, from my own experience of speaking to many groups about Christian community, that nothing arouses the ire of Americans, and especially church members, like saying that there is nothing that can be done. It is the ultimate foolishness to the world, but it may be the beginning of the wisdom of God.

Community is a by-product of the Spirit. Setting out to create community will not create community. As a leader in the charismatic movement and a writer on Christian community put it, Christian community is not built by building Christian community.[9] Community is the side result of doing something else, like following the leading of the Spirit. In more antiseptic terms, a group of psychologists studying community report the same thing: "The act of building a physical community is not adequately cohesive to hold people together . . . the members begin living together . . . before they have a community."[10] The disciples of Jesus did not sit down in a board meeting in the upper room with a blueprint of how to build community. When the Spirit came, community was created in their midst. The nineteenth-century evangelicals did not determine that community was the best way to meet their needs and set about organizing. They felt naturally drawn together by their experiences of the Spirit. The Shakers, the Mormons, the Oneida brethren had tremendous organizational skills, but they put these at the service of strengthening the community that the Spirit had created. They did not create the community in the first place. The primary goal of the first participants in the Catholic charismatic revival was not to start communities but to follow the Spirit as they felt led. Out of the context created by their exercising the spiritual gifts, praying together, and reading the scripture, community was born naturally. One of them recalls:

> One of the earliest realizations among the participants in the charismatic wildfire which burst forth among American Catholics in the winter of 1967 was the need for community life. . . . We gathered frequently because we sensed that our growth depended on it. We have come to understand that this formation of Spirit-led communities was no accident. Whenever the Lord pours out his Holy Spirit, he draws men together in unity.[11]

The Catholic charismatic communities at Notre Dame and Ann Arbor are very tightly organized, but this organization grew out of their experiences of community, it did not create them.

In more theological language, the basic insight of the New Testament and the charismatic experience regarding community is that community is formed by the Spirit not the law. The law is a series of demands laid upon one. Whenever someone comes to the church with a blueprint under his arm, whenever someone tells you that if you only do these ten things then you will have community, they are

preaching the law. Following the law is too easy. It is what
our pride wants. It is what the world wants from us—a
technique, an infallible solution. Following the law is
counterproductive. The law feeds our pride. If we followed
someone's directions and set out to build Christian community on our own, we'd soon find ourselves saying, "Look
what we're doing, we are building community." We would
turn and look at ourselves and away from the working of
the Spirit, which alone creates community.

Paul says Christians are freed from the law but it is a
paradoxical freedom. It is freedom for a more terrible
obligation than the law imposes—the obligation to follow
the Spirit. There are no techniques for building community
except that paradoxical negation of all technique—waiting
upon the Spirit. As St. Paul, and Luther after him, found
out, the law only throws one back upon oneself. Rather
than providing that self-transcendence, which can nourish
community, the law and its demands keep one wiggling in
the coils of one's self regard: Am I doing the right thing? Am
I working as hard as I ought to? There are no programs or
techniques for self-denial, nor can any law demand it. Thus
no programs or laws create koinonia. One cannot demand
of others that, by their own power, they free themselves
from themselves. By turning them back on their own
power, they are forced to concentrate on the very thing
from which they are seeking to turn. Programs, laws,
techniques, all throw the individual back upon himself and
his own efforts. They may be therapeutic but they cannot
create community.

Only the Spirit can create community, because only the
Spirit can create people who can live in community. Only
by becoming aware of a power and vision beyond oneself
can one transcend oneself. To rely on one's own self to get

out of one's self is contradictory. People who gather in response to some demand are usually hung up on their own efforts. People who gather to meet their own needs usually fall into mutual masturbation. People who are aware that they are part of something larger than themselves are, by the very experience of being humble before that greater reality, formed into community. In humility, the renunciation of the needs of self, not for the self's sake but for the sake of something beyond the self, one gains the self-transcendence necessary for community. Thus, humility is a part of the creation of community. Christianity has always said that conversion and the creation of community are the work of the Spirit. How could it be otherwise? If they were something man did, they would be only another form of human self-aggrandizement.

What can be said to those Christians who hunger after community and desire the renewal of the church? Are they to sit back passively and wait for God to miraculously hand them a community? The answer must be yes and no. They ought to wait upon the Lord, but waiting on the Lord is not something passive. The same pattern can be discerned in the disciples prior to the day of Pentecost, the foundation of the early monastic orders, the first evangelical communes, and the beginning of the Catholic charismatic communities. In every case, people were drawn to one another and so they waited upon the Lord *together*. When they were together they prayed together; and for the early Christians and the Pentecostals (and perhaps some of the nineteenth-century evangelical groups) this included exercising the spiritual gifts. Most of these groups searched the Scriptures together for common guidance. To break the headlong rush after technique and useless activity the answer to those who seek community must first be the injunction to stop and to wait. But for Christians, waiting upon the Lord is an active not a passive waiting. Meeting together, praying together, seeking and exercising spiritual gifts together, searching the Scriptures together is the pattern that characterized the waiting on the Spirit that led to the creation of Christian community, from the first Christians through the early monasteries, the evangelical communes, and the Pentecostals.

After the initial experience of community, certain forms and structures can strengthen and nourish it. Rejecting technique in favor of reliance on the Spirit's work is not intended to imply that community has no form. A body needs a skeleton to give it strength and shape and enable it to do its work. A growing community needs structure for the same reason. Paul says that certain offices (pastors, teachers, prophets, etc.) are part of the Spirit's gift to build up the body. A body must take some form and the Body of Christ must take the form of Christ. Paul indicates that there are some things that must be done if the body, once created, is to be built up in Christ's image (teaching, administration, prophecy, works of service, miracles, etc.). These come into play after the basic experience of koinonia, to enable it to take shape. I, and many others, have written about the things that are necessary to sound growth in community.[12] It is not important to repeat them, for the point here is that community is given its *birth* only by the Spirit and not by human technique. After it is born, then the best wisdom available must be used to nourish and form it.

Community is a key by-product of the Spirit's work. As the search for community was beginning in America in the sixties, the charismatic movement was recovering for the church the connection between community and the Holy

Spirit. Responding to the communal movement, churches ought to examine their congregational lives by the standard of New Testament koinonia. Community is basic to Christian experience; its formation is central to carrying out God's plan. A Spirit-formed community is a major context in which people encounter the Spirit. But such koinonia will always remain paradoxical in the eyes of the world, since it demands getting outside of oneself, the abnegation of pride, and the rejection of technique. From the charismatics the church must learn that only the Spirit creates community. Churches can take a lead in the search for community, for, empowered by the Spirit, they can unpack any paradoxes of community and set forth the experience out of which community is fashioned. Christians are experiencing the creation of community but only among those who are willing to accept the paradoxes of such community. A charismatic understanding of community reveals not only why it is central to Christianity but also why it will remain forever paradoxical or, as Paul says, "foolish" in the eyes of the world.

2
The Kingdom and the Spirit

The coming of the Spirit convinced the disciples that the Kingdom of God was about to arrive. Jesus had come to say that the Kingdom of God was at hand; his mission was not simply to discuss the Kingdom but to proclaim its nearness. The Kingdom is at the door; it is arriving finally. "If by the Spirit of God I cast out demons, then the Kingdom of God has come upon you," Jesus tells the expectant crowds. There is a note of finality about this. Jesus' preaching was not abstract discourse about the nature of the Kingdom nor ethical teaching about how to construct it. It was the blunt message that the Kingdom had appeared.

THE IDEA OF THE KINGDOM

A sense of urgency flavors the Gospels. The Kingdom has arrived, the end is soon to come. Mark constantly uses the word "immediately" and Matthew and Luke echo his statement that "truly there are some standing here who will not taste death before they see the Kingdom come with power." This urgency is picked up by Luke in the saying that "no one who puts his hand to the plow and looks back is fit for the Kingdom of God." It is reinforced by numerous demands for watchfulness lest the Lord return at any moment. "Take heed. Watch. For you know not when the time will come . . ." begins one passage in Mark which ends, ". . . and what I say to you I say to all, watch." Matthew tells of ten virgins, five who were wisely on guard and five who foolishly forgot to keep watch. Jesus' sense of the imminence of the Kingdom is heightened by this constant call to be on the lookout for it.

The Pentecostal experience of the early church fortified this expectation. The prophet Joel had said that a special outpouring of the Spirit would be a sign of the end of time. The Christians seized on their experience as a fulfillment of that prophecy. St. Paul did not often speak of the Kingdom, but it is clear that the expectation of a final manifestation of the reign of God is not foreign to his thoughts. Paul connects the event of Pentecost directly with the expectation of the Kingdom. This special gift of the Spirit is, he says, the first installment of the coming Kingdom. It guarantees us that the Kingdom is on its way and gives us a foretaste of what it will be (2 Cor. 1:22, 5:5; Eph. 1:14). Paul presupposes that, in the experience of the Spirit, Christians glimpse the future reign of God. The Spirit-filled community gives them an idea of what life in the Kingdom will be like.

Like the term koinonia, the idea of the Kingdom is not as prominent in the postapostolic writings as it is in the New Testament. The emphasis shifts away from the immediacy of the Kingdom coming by God's power toward a definition of the Kingdom as the ethical behavior of the Christian assemblies. In those fathers of the church who speak of the Kingdom it often means a collection of those who live morally. Following beside this tendency is an increasing identification of the Kingdom with the church. Paul said that life in the community was a foretaste of the Kingdom but it was not the Kingdom fully come. There remains in Paul an unresolved tension between the Kingdom breaking in upon the first Christians through the pouring out of the Spirit and the fact that history is still going on and the Kingdom has not completely arrived. But if the Kingdom is simply a name for the congregation of moral men, it is more easily identified with the church. These trends climax in Augustine, who identifies the city of God, running throughout history, with the church and thus paves the way for the medieval church to see itself as the incarnation of the Kingdom of God upon the earth.

The Reformation brought a new wave of impatient expectation of the Kingdom. The crisis of events—the medieval order crumbling into disunity, the rise of new churches, the expansion of economic opportunities—all lent credence to the feeling that something totally new was about to happen. Men poured over their Bibles and diligently examined every event for its prophetic significance. The sixteenth century in Europe and the seventeenth century in England saw the rise of radical millenarian groups who sought to hasten the Kingdom by violent revolution. While abhorring such sectarians, the orthodox Lutherans and Calvinists shared their fervent hope that the Reformation and the overthrow of the church of Rome marked the beginning of the end.

Nowhere was this zeal more evident than in America. Feeling that they were living in the twilight of history and that the churches were not sufficiently pure to do justice to the end times, the Puritans left England to carry out a further purifying of the church. The reformation was dragging its heels in England and they hoped to outflank its slow progress. By creating truly reformed churches in America they would show the rest of the world the way. In the course of the seventeenth century, when the reformation took other turns and refused to follow their lead, the New Englanders lost none of their sense of their own purity and righteousness. But they shifted the emphasis from Europe to America. Rather than being guiding lights to purify the churches of other nations, they turned inward and their own land became the locus of their interest. America, which contained the purest churches, was to be the scene of the final drama of history. Cotton Mather was sure the New Jerusalem was to arrive in America, built upon the foundations of his Puritan forefathers. Half a century later, in the midst of an unexpected kindling of the fires of religion across the colonies, Jonathan Edwards thought he saw the Kingdom of God coming in America, brought about by the first great awakening.

The fires of revival died down as the eighteenth century closed, but they burst into flame again during the beginning of the nineteenth century. This revival, too, reactivated a multitude of ideas about the Kingdom. William Miller, a revivalist, and his followers calculated that the world would end in 1843. The world did not end but the Adventist church began with its teaching that the Kingdom of God might come any time. The Mormons preserved the faith of Cotton Mather that the Kingdom would come first in America and set out west to build the New Jerusalem. But the great leaders of the second great awakening, like Charles Finney and Theodore Weld, felt that the revivals were not a sign of the Kingdom's coming but a cause of it. To them the Kingdom meant the moral reformation of the world and the revival was to inspire men to get to work to change the society. To be converted in the revival was to convert to a whole host of holy causes. Temperance societies, women's rights' leagues, antislavery parties all flourished in the wake of the revival and newly saved souls were channeled by Finney and Weld and others into these groups. The end of the antislavery movement, the Civil War, and the rise of individual capitalism and industrialism, with problems that seemed intractable to societies of Bible-waving saints, put a stop to this combination of revivalism and social reform. The churches embraced the gospel of individualism and set about enhancing themselves as institutions.

At the same time that the practical politics of the Kingdom were dying out in America the idea of the Kingdom was being rediscovered in Germany. German biblical scholarship turned a critical eye on the Bible and realized that the key to Jesus' preaching was the Kingdom of God. This discovery provoked an almost constant dispute among advocates of different interpretations of the Kingdom. The liberal scholars of the nineteenth century saw the Kingdom as an ethical stance; Jesus was referring to the Kingdom of moral men. The greatest of their spokesmen, Adolph Harnack, said, "In the combination of these ideas—God the Father, Providence, the position of men as God's children, the infinite value of the human soul—the whole Gospel is expressed." More pietistic students of the New Testament rejected the liberals' moralizing and suggested the Kingdom had mystical overtones; Jesus was referring to a Kingdom within the soul of each man. Others, like Albert Schweitzer, tried to see

Jesus in the context of his own times, when, they argued, everyone expected the end of the world. To them the Kingdom was something alien and apocalyptic; Jesus was referring to the end of history.

Most Americans were not interested in the speculations of German scholars; few were interested in the idea of the Kingdom of God at all. Some Americans continued in the Adventist movement after the failure of William Miller's predictions. Throughout the nineteenth and early twentieth centuries they organized conferences and published tracts equating the Kingdom of God with Christ's return at the end of time. Others, in whom the fires of revival still burned, sought the Kingdom of God in the hearts of individuals warmed by the flames of tent meetings and pulpit-thumping preachers. Still others saw in the idea of the Kingdom a way in which the church could confront the problems of industrialization and urbanization.

In the 1890s a few ministers, working in churches at the core of the urban blight that was creeping across the American countryside, realized that the individualistic gospel of American Christianity made no sense out of the realities of workers crushed under the wheels of giant corporations or driven into poverty by the fluctuations of impersonal economic laws. In conferences and pamphlets men like Washington Gladden and Walter Rauschenbusch tried to forge a "social Christianity," which repudiated individualism and confronted the collective problems of mankind. In 1892, Rauschenbusch organized a group called the Brotherhood of the Kingdom, which took as its goal transforming industrial society into the Kingdom of God.

For Rauschenbusch and his followers, the Kingdom of God was a sociopolitical reality. It represented Jesus' vision of a new social order. Because God's Kingdom was a political kingdom, the social gospel ministers urged their churches into political action. They provided social services, they supported union organizing, they lobbied on behalf of social legislation. In his optimism, Rauschenbusch saw the Kingdom as a moral possibility: If committed men would work together they could bring the Kingdom to earth. The tools Rauschenbusch chose were primarily the secular tools of the social sciences. He had faith in research and planning, in economics, social work, and politics. For Rauschenbusch the church was a social service institution like the clinic, the school, or the trade union, and its function was much the same as theirs.

The social gospel movement stirred a great controversy over differing ideas of the Kingdom of God. In opposition to the social gospel and other liberal currents in American Christianity, those who defined the Kingdom as the end of time joined with those who felt it in the heart of each converted soul. Out of their agreement that the Kingdom of God had nothing to do with economics and politics, the Fundamentalistic movement was born. This attack on the liberals was launched in a series of twelve books called *The Fundamentals;* they contain no articles on the Kingdom of God *per se* and the parts that deal with the future look forward only to a cataclysmic return of Christ, which will destroy and not transform the present creation.

The present-day American church inherits these radically opposed definitions of the Kingdom of God and all its attempts to think through its relation to society oscillate between these two poles. The social gospel transforms the Kingdom of God into political power directed toward certain goals; the Evangelical sees the Kingdom as an otherworldly, spiritual reality, which should not be contaminated by the ambiguities of politics. The social kingdom comes through political action; the Evangelical kingdom comes through individual conversion and has little time to be deflected by political involvement. During the sixties and seventies the sons of the social gospel called on the church to support civil rights demonstrations and then welfare reform; the sons of the Fundamentals responded by asking what the Kingdom of God had to do with legal battles and economic policy, what expertise had the church to speak on courtroom tactics and tax structures? Some of the grandsons of the social gospel are feeling a sense of failure as political action continues to fall short of the Kingdom of God; some of the grandsons of the Fundamentals are developing an uneasy conscience. The first seek for "the spiritual dimensions of the political struggle," so-called by a recent conference in Britain; the second try to fashion an Evangelical social ethic. Perhaps the two will meet in the center, but this is not likely as long as both remain trapped by the assumption that the Kingdom of God must be either a political platform or an apocalyptic event.

KINGDOM AND COMMUNITY

American social ethics have always begun with the idea of the Kingdom of God. A new direction in social ethics and the church's social strategy might begin with a new look at the Kingdom. For St. Paul, understanding the Kingdom begins with our experiencing the Spirit, for it is the Spirit that gives us a taste of the nature of the Kingdom. The sensitivity to the Spirit in the charismatic movement can generate insight into the nature of the Kingdom, which, in turn, will produce its own social ethics and strategy.

Saying the Spirit gives us a foretaste of the Kingdom implies that we can deduce something of the nature of the Kingdom from the working of the Spirit. A large part of the Spirit's work is creating community. Each is given the gifts of the Spirit for the common good, the Spirit is poured out that the body may be built up. Paul's famous metaphor of the church as a body comes in the middle of his discussion of spiritual gifts. The church is a kind of "spiritual body," a body animated by the Spirit. Paul distinguishes the gifts (1 Cor. 12) and the fruits (Gal. 5) of the Spirit. The fruits are the ethical form the Spirit takes among his people, just as the gifts are the functional forms of the Spirit within the body. The gifts are certain offices within the body, the fruits are styles of living within the body. The fruits of the Spirit listed by Paul are almost all corporate or social. They are the qualities necessary for people to live together in community. The fruits of the Spirit are contrasted with the works of the flesh. The works of the flesh are those qualities that make trouble for community life; they are all things that create schism in the body. People who "live in the flesh" are those who cannot live in community; people who live in the Spirit are those who can grow together in a body.

In the New Testament, the Spirit is seen as a corporate Spirit, working to incorporate new parts into the body. Manifesting himself, not for the sake of individuals but for the common good, his gifts are for the invigoration of community. The Kingdom, of which one has a foretaste in the work of the Spirit, is a corporate, a social kingdom. In opposing the exaggerated individualism of much of modern American Protestantism, the social gospel writers were correct in emphasizing the corporate nature of the Kingdom.

The Kingdom, however, is not characterized by the exercise of coercion or manipulation or any of the other forces that seem to govern man's life in society. Many have remarked upon the fact that in the Gospels Jesus does not offer any platform for political activity. He seems almost oblivious to the issues of power that govern the lives of those among whom he moves. There seems no conclusive evidence that he associated with the zealots or any others who saw the issues of life wholly in political terms. Certainly those who knew him best never sensed that he intended his message to be interpreted in political categories. The Gospel of John records Jesus' saying that his kingdom is not of this world. This might be interpreted eschatologically (and thus in line with the Synoptics) to mean that Jesus' Kingdom is not of this present age but belongs to the age to come. Or it might be interpreted more Platonically to mean that his Kingdom is a spiritual reality in contrast to the physical reality of mundane existence. In either case, a tension is here revealed that cuts through the entire New Testament and that is best expressed in John's Gospel by the saying, "you are in the world but not of it." The Kingdom of God is in the world but it is not a worldly Kingdom.

Paul maintains the same tension in different terms. He contrasts the life in the Spirit with what he calls life in the flesh. This is not a Platonic dualism. Life in the flesh is not simply physical life. Life in the Spirit, too, is life in the body. Even the resurrected life will be embodied life. It is life lived from the Spirit not the flesh. It is life that is rooted in the Spirit of God and from this root grow the fruits of the Spirit. It is life that expresses this Spirit through the gifts of the Spirit and the fruits of the Spirit, which are the embodiments of the Spirit in the life of mankind. Thus there is the same tension between being in the world but not of it. Life in the Spirit is life in the body but it is not life in the flesh. Paul tells his congregations not to live in the flesh but he also tells them they can't avoid living in the world and that they shouldn't try to separate themselves from the world. They must live in the world but not be conformed to it.

Life in the flesh, Paul says, is characterized by such things as groups at war with one another, fierce competition, rivalry, creation of dissension, and setting up conflicting parties. This is a pretty good description of man's political life as it has been experienced in the Western world. Politics then, with its manipulation, coercion, setting one group against another, is a manifestation of the kingdom of the flesh. By implication, then, it has no place in the Kingdom of God. In the Synoptic Gospels Jesus contrasts the social life of the nations of the world with that of the Kingdom of God. The Gentiles, he says, lord their authority over others, but it must not be so among you. Your leaders must be your servants. He is implying that the opposite of the political life in the world is what must prevail in the Kingdom of God. We might extrapolate and say, "the people of the world run for office but it should not be so among you," or "the people of the world set up parties but it must not be so among you."

The Kingdom of God stands in opposition to the ways of the present world, while being present in the world. The Kingdom is spiritual not political, yet it encompasses man's political life. Life in the Spirit is lived in this world but it is not of this world. It exists in this age while expressing the age to come. The Kingdom of God is a social reality, but it is not a political one (i.e., it does not involve coercion, manipulation, and partisan strife). Any attempt to negate these tensions by making the Kingdom of God into either another worldly kingdom or into something so spiritual that it becomes irrelevant to the world for which Christ died is to destroy the fundamental character of the Kingdom and the Gospel. This tension is the axis around which the whole Gospel revolves: the Kingdom is in the world but not of it, life in the Spirit is lived in the body, Christ was in the world, as are all men, and yet was equal with God.

However, the very term Kingdom of God is a political one. It obviously refers to the rule of God over his creation. The Kingdom is the place where God reigns. Doesn't this mean that the Kingdom is necessarily something political? This is the question of *how* does God rule. The question that is usually raised in relation to the Kingdom is the question of *what* does God rule. This is the wrong question, for there can only be one answer given. God rules everything, that is what it means to call him Lord. Politics, economics, one's private life, all must stand over the Lordship of One who is truly God. Those who want to make the Kingdom into something otherworldly, or to confine it to the private sector, miss this most fundamental theological fact. If Jesus is called Lord, then he must be Lord over all aspects of life. Those who would limit the Gospel to the private world thereby subtly deny the Lordship of Christ. The Kingdom which he brings cannot be identified with a laissez-faire attitude or a policy of "hands off" the world. The rule of Christ is not confined to the private sphere.

The question, then, is not the question of what does God rule. He rules over all. The question is, *how* does God rule? Since the controversy in America over the social gospel movement, two answers have been given, which flow from two different views of the Kingdom. One says that God rules through private individuals. This is the answer of those who emphasize the Kingdom's not being of the world. Not being of the world means not being contaminated by the sinfulness of power and the ambiguities of policy but being safely nestled in the private lives of individuals. To these people the church is a collection of individuals with the Kingdom in their hearts. The other side emphasizes the Kingdom's being in the world. Being in the world means being like every institution in the world and so the church is seen as a corporate structure struggling alongside other similar institutions, such as political parties or trade unions, to achieve certain common ends.

The first answer seems to reflect a sociological naïveté about the inevitability of institutionalization and the effects of society upon the faithful. Throughout history the most ethereal of movements have had to take on some structure in response to the inevitable pressures of their society upon them. Every group is formed to some extent along the contours of its culture. The church can be a better witness to its not being of the world when it does not try to hide from itself the ways in which it is in fact in the world. More important, this sectarian rejection of the world implies a distortion in the foundation of Christianity, it denies the Lordship of Jesus Christ over the world and confines his activities to a single narrow sphere of his creation. In opposing the social gospel, the Fundamentals discussed the Kingdom only as a cataclysmic possibility at the end of time; it had nothing to do with the historical world. In the New Testament, the Kingdom is never seen as that otherworldly. The message of Jesus was precisely the opposite, the Kingdom of God is at hand! It is now breaking in and transforming all of life under the Lordship of Christ. Paul says that Christians this side of the Second Coming experience this transformation and this new society. The Pietistic view of the Kingdom truncates the church. In the New Testament the church is not a loose federation of redeemed atoms but is a communal body.

The answer of the social gospel is strong where the Pietists are weak. But it identifies the way of God too simply with the ways of men. The Kingdom of God becomes just another power structure in the society. The Pietists can never give a comprehensive theological answer to the ways in which the Kingdom is in the world, the social gospel can never find words to discuss the fact that the Kingdom is not of the world. When the Kingdom is identified with a human political program and that program falls far short of the perfection expected of the Kingdom of God, the social gospeler becomes discouraged and is tempted to give up. The power, which is supposedly the sign of the Kingdom, becomes dissipated, as it is hard to discern the power of God amid the ruins of political programs.

COMMUNITY AND SOCIAL RESPONSIBILITY

In one sense this debate within American Protestantism over which is primary, individual regeneration or social change, which has been going on for almost a century, is a reflection of the almost classical debate in Western social science between psychology and sociology, between those who study the individual and those who study the social matrix of human life. In some ways it is paralleled by another debate over the effects of heredity and environment. Usually these debates have been resolved by the simple suggestion that they are both (equally) important. This may be quite true but an attempt to reconcile the individual and corporate dimensions of human experience by a balancing act will not contribute to an understanding of the Kingdom of God. The Kingdom of God is neither a collection of redeemed but isolated individuals nor a totalitarian state. It is koinonia, a style of existence all its own, which encompasses the private and social aspects of life.

We have precious few images to describe koinonia and, therefore, the Kingdom. Our society serves up to us almost no experiences or models of community. We are surfeited with the language of the intensely private and personal; at its best our political system is zealous for the rights of individuals. We have also been treated to gruesome images of concern for the corporate and the societal rushing into totalitarian oppression, but we lack any experience of koinonia, a spiritual unity where each member retains its integrity while remaining a responsible part of the whole.

Lacking the experience of community, our politics and social ethics are bankrupt. Politically we vacillate between anarchy and totalitarianism. The slogans of the new left move from anarchy to participatory democracy to an elitist dictatorship telling the people what is best for them. Conservatives formerly saw themselves as guardians of American individualism, now, under the rhetoric of law and order, they advocate building up massive concentrations of military and police power in the central government—always historically the first step toward totalitarianism. Economically we seem doomed to oscillate between the models of private capitalism and state socialism. Yet we no longer live in the world of Adam Smith, for most of our economic resources are concentrated in the hands of a few sectors of the economy, which are heavily dependent upon government fiscal policy, regulative authority, and contracts for survival. Nor can classical socialism order the subtleties of the complex technological economics that have developed in the West. The church, too, stumbles between these two poles. For awhile the sons of the social gospel are in control and the church becomes a social institution pursuing political goals. Then the sons of the Fundamentals try to pull Christianity back into being an inward, private piety, where the church becomes a body so mystical as to be hidden from the world for which Christ died. In its staggering back and forth, the church mirrors a society it has failed to redeem and so trips over its chief cornerstone, and its social ethics lie in ruins. Only by gaining some glimpse of the reality of community can these social problems be tackled. Perhaps only the church, if it recaptures its life as a koinonia, can point the way back to community and bring some harmony out of the endless warfare between the private and the corporate.

If the church can give the world an example of koinonia, it will do more toward healing the problem of society than by any program it might undertake. From this taste of community, economists and political scientists might mine a new economics and politics of community, which would overcome the dilemmas represented by capitalism or socialism, anarchy or totalitarianism. In contributing thus to the healing of the world, the church would also heal itself. Living in community would teach people a balance between individual experience and corporate responsibility. "He who would gain his life must lose it" is part of the paradox of community. In koinonia the individual's needs are fulfilled and they become themselves without loss of any of their personal integrity. Yet they are also pointed beyond selfishness to their brothers and sisters and they are freed from their hang-ups in order to love others. In koinonia one does not lose oneself in the mass—that is totalitarianism; nor does one withdraw from responsibility for others—that is moral sectarianism.

Koinonia would also push the church beyond the sterile options of the Fundamentals versus the social gospel. The New Testament church existed in the midst of the world;

Paul condemned the Corinthians' refusal to associate with worldly men. Empowered and supported by community, the early Christians were not sucked in by the pagan society and were able to resist its illegitimate encroachments on their lives. They were in the world but not of it. Community enabled them to live and work in the world without being vitiated. Living in community would enable modern Christians to proclaim the Lordship of Christ without either identifying his Kingdom with some human and penultimate program or ideology (as the social gospel did, and which the authors of the Fundamentals rightly rejected), or making it so otherworldly as to deny the Lordship of Christ over the very world he came to redeem (as the sectarians did, and which the social gospel rightly condemned).

In the seventies the church has reached an impasse: some Evangelicals, troubled by their "uneasy consciences," are seeking to forge an Evangelical social ethic, some former social gospelers are seeking for the spiritual and theological roots of social ethics. At the same time, a search for community has been calling on the church to rediscover its basic style of life and the charismatic movement has been recovering for the church the power of the Spirit. *Forming community has been the social strategy of the Spirit since the day of Pentecost; Paul says it is the very plan of God. Allowing the Spirit to create community in its midst and throughout the world must become part of the social mission of the church.*

HOW THE KINGDOM COMES

What is the relation between this building of community and the coming of the Kingdom of God? The debate swirling around the social gospel movement as to whether the Kingdom could be defined in political terms derived its practical importance from the strategic problem of the Kingdom's coming. If the Kingdom is a political entity, it can be ushered in by political means. Defining the Kingdom politically logically led the social gospel movement to view the church as a pressure group, which used all the channels of power to achieve its goal of bringing the Kingdom. The authors of the Fundamentals, in rejecting the social gospel, said the Kingdom would not come until the end of history, when God in his sovereignty would roll up the rug of time and miraculously and instantaneously build the New Jerusalem. In dwelling on the most miraculous and extraordinary aspects of the Second Coming, the Fundamentals imply that there is nothing for man to do. The church is a collection of those who are waiting patiently for his coming.

The early preaching of the Gospel had little to do with how men might bring the Kingdom. The primitive church's message simply stated that God was at work and the Kingdom was coming. The question was not, would the Kingdom come, but only what role people would have vis-à-vis its arrival. Would they be part of its coming or a hindrance to it? The response to this message was not simply accepting it and then quietly waiting. Acceptance of the Gospel meant giving oneself over to the working of God and being used for his purposes. The gifts of the Spirit (healing, teaching, evangelizing, etc.) are active. In rediscovering these spiritual gifts, the Pentecostals realized that surrendering to the Spirit meant allowing the Spirit to work through one as he did through the disciples. The baptism in the Holy Spirit meant becoming zealous for the Kingdom, just as Paul was. The Pentecostals uncovered the early Christian proclamation that God is working his purposes out through his Spirit and if people give themselves to that Spirit they can share in his work.

Pentecostal churches were right in emphasizing that the dispensation of the Spirit was an integral part of God's plan. The Spirit ties the building of community together with the coming of the Kingdom. But the Pentecostals were unable to see the social and cosmic dimensions of God's plan. This narrowing of the Pentecostal focus to the individual was probably due to the heritage of individualism, which classical Pentecostalism received from American evangelicalism. Paul argues that God's plan is not simply to save individual souls but to fill all things with himself so that at the end he will be "all in all." God does this by filling all things with his Spirit. Christ ascended in order to fill all things with himself by giving his gifts to men. These gifts Paul mentions are for the building up of the community. The Spirit is to form community. This Spirit-filled community is both a foretaste of the Kingdom and a means to its realization. Through the work of the community of the Spirit more of life is filled with the Spirit and this is a further step in God's plan of filling all things with himself.

The Kingdom is the rule of God and God rules in Spirit. ✶ The Kingdom will not come by political means but only by the working of the Spirit. But when, and as, it comes, it brings *all* things into subjection to Christ—the political, the economic, the intellectual, as well as the private spheres of life. And it transforms all of these spheres, for it is not of this world and therefore cannot be identified with any of the kingdoms of this world, neither the ideologies men call Western democracy nor Eastern communism nor any combination of them. To say that the Kingdom does not come through politics, economics, or technology does not mean the Kingdom has nothing to do with the political, economic, or technological orders. Clearly it does, for it will transform all of these into subjection to Christ. It is only to say that these orders are not primary in God's plan. Individuals are not primary either (except in the sense that all experience happens to individuals, not to isolated individuals but to members of communities and societies). What is primary in the plan of God is the koinonia, the community and the Kingdom, which transcends individualism and collectivism and encompasses both the public and the private realms of life.

Does this mean God rules only through his Spirit? No. He also rules through creation and providence and through the institutions and structures established under his creation and providence. Many Pentecostals who become fascinated with the rule of God through the Spirit neglect the rule of God through creation and providence. Nature, society, and the historical process tend to be ignored and the Lordship of God over these areas is played down theologically. Too great an emphasis on God's rule through his Spirit may tend to equate the Spirit-filled community with the Kingdom as the only place where God rules. Thus sectarianism often sprouts after the showers of God's Spirit. The only theological antidote to this is an emphasis on the rule of God through creation and providence equal to that on the rule of God through the gifts of the Spirit, or emphasizing that the gifts of the Spirit perfect nature, they do not negate it.

Since man is a self-conscious being, in order for the rule of God to be fully manifest in the human realm, man must self-consciously give himself to this rule. The koinonia is formed when men self-consciously submit to the rule of God, especially the rule of God through his Spirit. The koinonia is not the Kingdom *per se*. It is, however, a foretaste of the Kingdom in that it is the place where the rule of God is consciously experienced, acknowledged, and lived out. The community cannot be identified with the Kingdom (as the sectarian tradition does), since the rule of God embraces more than just the Spirit-filled community. But the koinonia is the presence of the Kingdom among men and nations since it is where the rule of God is freely acknowledged.

The ruling of the Godhead can be conceived as a series of concentric circles. The outer circle is the rule of God the Father in creation and providence, encompassing the whole cosmos. The middle circle is the reign of Christ, which takes place within the larger context of the divine creation and providence but will not, until the end when "all things are put in subjection under his feet," coincide with creation. Within this circle is the third and smallest one which represents the work of the Spirit—the Spirit-filled community, which acknowledges the Lordship of God the Father and the Lordship of Christ. When the Kingdom comes, all these circles will be one. As a doctrine of the Trinity this is plainly inadequate, for all three are involved in creation, providence, redemption, and the consummation of history. However, this clearly illustrates two New Testament themes: that the work of Christ takes place in the larger context created by the work of creation. In a way the classical doctrine of the Trinity does not, this scheme maintains the New Testament witness to a special work of the Spirit within the body of Christ.

The coming of the Kingdom can be seen as the progression of the inner circles toward the outer rim until all the cosmos is subject to Christ and filled with the Spirit, thus clarifying the problem central to the disputes over the kingdom in the American church. By what strategy will the Kingdom ever come? The Kingdom will come only through the submission of all life to the Lordship of Christ (through the preaching of the Gospel) and being filled with the Spirit (through being transformed into community). Through the Gospel and the community the Spirit hastens the time when all things will be subject to Christ and filled with the presence of God and the three circles will converge at the outer rim.

POLITICS AND THE KINGDOM

What role, then, does politics play? Sectarians, such as sixteenth-century Anabaptists, completely separated the Kingdom of God from the political kingdoms of this world by identifying the rule of God only with his rule over the community. Because they believed the world would always reject the Gospel, they sought to become islands of holiness in a sea of immorality. The sectarians mitigated the Lordship of Christ by confining it to the church. They also undercut the paradox of the Gospel by making the Lordship of Christ over the world only a future possibility, rather than something that is both present and also yet to come. Those who have affirmed the being of the church *in* the world by identifying the Gospel with some worldly ideology of the left or the right undermine the Gospel paradox from the other side. They deny the church's not being of the world. Koinonia will provide a way to affirm the Lordship of Christ over all of life and keep the church from the sectarian's total rejection of the world, while also distinguishing the Kingdom of God from man's political kingdoms.

Rejection of politics as a means to bring the Kingdom may deny the Lordship of Christ or it may affirm it. The

Christian might withdraw from politics (i.e., from the process of manipulation, coercion, etc.) and yet affirm the Lordship of Christ over the political realm if he does those things that will further the building up of the body of Christ and therefore the coming of the Kingdom and the Lordship of Christ over the world. The basic question is—will the Kingdom come by political means? Nowhere does the Gospel or the history of the church suggest that it will! Nowhere does the Bible imply that the programs of men usher in the Kingdom of God!

What, then, are people to do? They are to do those things the Spirit gives them to do: preach, teach, heal, reconcile and restore, judge and admonish. In other words, live that Christian life of service in the Spirit, which builds up the Body of Christ and carries on its work. The goal of one's actions must be to serve God and let him worry about bringing the Kingdom. The aim must be the service of God's work, not one's own. If one separates oneself from the political kingdoms of the world simply for the sake of withdrawing, out of fear of the world or some other such motive, one is implicitly denying the Lordship of Jesus Christ over the world. If one withdraws from the political kingdoms of the world in order to serve, in other ways, the plan of God, which will culminate in the Lordship of Jesus Christ over the world, then one is serving and not denying the Lordship of Jesus Christ. Withdrawing from politics does not mean withdrawing from the world. Serving God's plan in building up the body of Christ and extending the work of the Spirit-filled koinonia as a part of the coming Kingdom is not a rejection of the world. It is for the sake of the world and God's love for it that the body of Christ must be built up.

The people of God are still bidden to seek the peace of the

city in which they dwell (cf. Jer. 29:7) and to witness to the
Lordship of Jesus Christ over the whole of life. Therefore, a
total separation from the political kingdom of this world is
probably neither possible nor desirable. The political
process can serve the relative peace of the world. It also
stands under the Lordship of Jesus Christ. This is subject to
the same paradox. The kingdoms of this world are, from
one standpoint, even now under the dominion of Christ but
this rule of Christ is yet to be fully manifest. From this
tension of the Kingdom present but not yet come arises the
Christian's duty not to neglect the political process. The
Christian has a duty to seek in the world as close an ap-
proximation to the will of Christ as possible. The continual
attempt to make it subject to the will of Christ is part of the
way that the Lordship of Christ is proclaimed over the
political process. The Christian knows that political activity
will not bring in the Kingdom of God nor undercut the
eschatological tension of the Kingdom of God, which, because it has not yet come, stands over and against the
human state of affairs. Therefore, politics is not his ultimate
concern. His primary concern must be submission to the
plan of God to fill all things with himself through his Spirit.
But political activity can serve to fulfill the biblical injunction to seek for peace and to proclaim the Lordship of
Christ over all.

CHARISM AND KINGDOM

How is the Christian's life of service in the Spirit to be
carried out? If the reception of the Spirit is one of the
distinguishing marks of Christianity, then what the New
Testament describes as the life in the Spirit is a description
of the Christian life. If the Christian life is a foretaste of the

Kingdom of God, then this life in the Spirit must give us some idea as to what will tie in with the Kingdom. In answer to a question about whether he is the one to bring the Kingdom, Jesus answers by listing a series of mighty deeds he has done. The sort of things he points to here are the same things that the disciples are described as doing in the synoptic accounts of the mission of the twelve and the seventy (healing, preaching, teaching, etc.). They are also the things that the Apostles are described as doing in the book of Acts and, by and large, they comprise Paul's list of gifts of the Spirit. The Christian life is not following laws or imitating a pattern. Rather it is following the leading of the Spirit and exercising the Spiritual gifts in witness, ministry, and mission. All the gifts of the Spirit are missionary. They are to be used to build up the body, serve the neighbor, give honor to Christ, and thereby carry out the plan of God.

However, there seems no reason to believe that Paul's specific list of the *charisms* (gifts) is exhaustive. Many things may be done today under the Spirit of wisdom and with the aim of love that were unheard of then (medicine, social work, counselling, etc.). God rules not only through the charisms but also through creation, through nature as well as through grace. Thus the plan of God can be advanced by these "natural" services being submitted to the Spirit. Since the charisms are clearly supernatural and these other services are the exercises of man's natural abilities, these are not the same as the charisms *per se*. But they can be legitimate extrapolations of the charisms if they are subject to the Body of Christ and the same tests of love, glorification of Christ, edification of the body, etc. Thus the church can be called to other forms of ministry besides (but not as substitutes for) the exercise of the charisms.

The question of incorporating new forms of ministry into the body may be a Catholic-Protestant dilemma. The

Catholic tradition (at least since Cardinal Newman) has recognized a principle of development within the church, its ministry, and dogmatic understanding within the limits of scriptural and historical continuity. The Protestant, with his sole reliance on the biblical norm, rarely allows for any development. Liberal Protestantism is an exception but it soon abandoned all limits of scriptural and historical continuity. The Protestant temptation is always to want to go back and play "first century" over again. The Pentecostals, being firmly Protestant, usually restrict the ministry of the Body to the specific charisms listed by Paul. This, when combined with a strong separation of grace from nature, may lead to a rejection of natural human means altogether. For the Catholic it is possible to incorporate modern techniques of medicine, social work, psychotherapy, etc. within the compass of the ministry—not as substitutes for, but as extensions of, the charismatic ministry.

The New Testament says that, through the Spirit, Christians share in the powers of the age to come. Therefore the manifestations of these powers in the works of Jesus, in the missions of the twelve and the seventy, in the deeds of the Apostles, and in the exercise of the gifts of the Spirit in the present, have eschatological, Kingdom-oriented significance. These are signs of the future Kingdom performed in the present. They not only give men a glimpse of the coming Kingdom but they hasten its arrival, as the sphere of the Spirit's work is enlarged.

It is not too difficult to conceive of individuals being filled with the Spirit, but at the end all of creation will be so. Can we conceive of institutions filled with the Spirit? Koinonia is itself an example of a corporate structure filled with the Spirit. Beyond that, communities of the Spirit are extending themselves and therefore the dominion of the Spirit into new areas. A charismatic community has taken over an abandoned inner-city parochial school and, since the community members give freely of their time and training, they can run the school for the benefit of the neighborhood children. Through them, children and their families are being touched with the Spirit. A charismatic parish in a decaying neighborhood has found its parishioners moving back into the city to live around the parish in community. Thus is the neighborhood being restored. Parishioners who are physicians, lawyers, teachers, and others run free clinics and services for the area. The Spirit's urban renewal is being carried out. A collection of Pentecostal households near a mental hospital are taking in patients who have either been given up by the staff or can live in a "halfway" situation. Through the healing power of the Spirit in community, many of these forgotten souls are being restored to useful life. These communities are not solving the vast problems of education, urban blight, or mental illness, but they point toward the time when schools, cities, and hospitals will be communities. Within the charismatic movement and the churches at large, physicians, nurses, teachers, social workers, businessmen, truck drivers, laborers are trying to bring something of the life of the Spirit into their work and to order their lives in such a way as to allow the Spirit to create community through them. As the perimeters of submission to the work of the Spirit are enlarged, more of existence is filled with the Spirit until that day comes when the earth shall be filled with the glory of God as the waters fill up the sea.

3

Experiencing and
Understanding

Born in an outpouring of the Spirit, the early church was
not only fired but also illuminated by the flames. The
church not only experienced the Spirit, it thought about
that experience. The Pentecostal explosion in the life of the
first Christians gave them new deeds and new feelings and
also new ideas. (The development of these ideas is discussed
in more detail in chapter 4.) These new ideas were not
created out of nothing. The disciples had only the
thought forms of their culture in which to understand their
experience. The Judaism of the early converts was a
multiplicity of groups formed by different influences. Each
group had developed its own ideas about the Spirit of God
before the day of Pentecost recorded in Acts. Those Jews
who remained dispersed beyond the borders of Palestine
imbibed various aspects of the dominant philosophy of the
day. For them, God was related to man through his Spirit
of wisdom, which they called by the Greek name *Sophia*.
Creation was formed on the pattern of God's wisdom.
Wisdom was not, however, only an idea; she was a

semidivine force spanning the gulf between man and God. Other Jews looked beyond the course of human history, which appeared to have run over the sons of Israel and confined them to an obscure eddy in the stream of events, to a final cataclysmic day when God would restore the nation of Israel. One of the signs of this great day would be the free flowing of God's Spirit, for the prophets foretold that in the final days "God would pour out his Spirit upon all flesh."

THE GROWING DOCTRINE OF THE SPIRIT

When those Jews who followed the carpenter of Nazareth received a dousing of God's Spirit unlike anything ever recorded in their history, it was natural for them to try to explain it in the terms of their heritage. Some seized on the speculations evolving around the divine wisdom and identified those categories with the Spirit of God. To them the Holy Spirit was a semidivine force mediating between the mind of God and the minds of men. They had received a double dose of the same Spirit that had aided in the creation of the world, led the children of Israel out of Egypt, and inspired the prophets of the Old Testament. Others took the first Pentecostal experience as a sign of the end. The Spirit is given to those who believe that the end is near and who accept Jesus as the harbinger of that end. On the day of Pentecost the Spirit fell only on the disciples, and when combined with the idea that the apocalyptic Spirit was only for the apocalyptic community, the first Pentecost created a tendency in early Christianity to limit the newly dispensed Spirit to the church. In the book of Acts, the Spirit is only promised to those who accept the ministry of Jesus (Acts 2:38; 5:32; 19:2-6); for Paul the basic function of the gifts of the Spirit is to build up the body of Christ (1 Cor. 12:4–11; 14:12; Eph. 4:11–12). On the other hand, the tradition of Hebrew wisdom universalized the work of the Spirit. The Spirit of God pervaded all things and was active in the creation of the world and the history of ancient Israel. Since the New Testament writers drew on many different categories in order to articulate their experience, there are conflicting tendencies in the biblical portrait of the Spirit. A universalizing tendency to see the Spirit as the Divine Presence in all creation pulls against a particularizing tendency to confine the Spirit to the church. An impetus toward continuity emphasizes the lineage of the New Testament Spirit with the kings and prophets of Israel; a consciousness of the uniqueness of the early Pentecostal experience drives some early Christians to speak of the Spirit as a special gift belonging only to Christians who, through Jesus, share in the powers of the new age.

The categories that the early Christians took from the synagogue into the church in order to speak of their experience had definite meanings that could not be totally erased. When the Spirit was identified with the Divine Wisdom, the Spirit was thereby pictured as a semidivine being or force. Both Jesus and the Spirit were called by the philosophical names used to describe a divine being or power. What was the relation between them? The confusion between Jesus and the Spirit in early Christian theology follows from a confusion in early Christian experience. Having known Jesus of Nazareth, the disciples now experienced the Spirit as well. The picture of Jesus calling the lame off their sickbeds, facing the Pharisees in heedless confrontation, etching his words into their lives, remained vivid in their minds. The Spirit was not just a continuation of that. The Spirit created his own universe of unknown languages, communities of love, and new forms of service. The animated world of the Spirit was not the same as the small circle of disciples trudging after the Master, but the energy that burst upon the disciples on Pentecost was, somehow, the same power that had drawn them to him. The new power of the Spirit was divine, just as Jesus was divine, and how better to describe this than to use the same language about the Spirit as one used about Jesus? But how, then, could you tell them apart?

The first Christians did not trouble themselves with these questions too much. Paul simply identified the Spirit with the resurrected Jesus (2 Cor. 3:17). Most of the early theologians followed Paul and equated the dispensation of the newly given Spirit with the recently crucified and resurrected Lord. But to identify the Spirit of God and the Son of God is to confuse their functions and make the world created by the Spirit simply a continuation of the work of the Son. Thus the Spirit soon became subordinated to the Son. This strengthened the tendency to limit the Spirit to the church. Since the Spirit was sent from the Son, he was only bestowed on those who followed Jesus. But this contradicted the images drawn from Hebrew wisdom theology, which universalized the Spirit's activity. To call the Spirit by the same name as the Son meant the Spirit, too, was a part of God and since God was present everywhere, his Spirit must be also.

Out of this development came, in A.D. 381, the classical formulation of the doctrine of the Trinity. Throughout the third and fourth centuries the developing church's theologians tried to articulate the Christian's experience of Jesus as a manifestation of God. Was he fully divine? Yes, the church answered. Since the same terms had been applied to the Spirit as to the Son, the outcome of the disputes applied equally to the Spirit. The Spirit, too, was divine. The classical doctrine of the Trinity cut through the confusion of the first four centuries by saying that the power manifest in the creation of the world, the love revealed in the work of Jesus, and the experiences created by the presence of the Spirit were three equal incursions of God into his world. Ironically, the problem, which began by too close an identification of the Spirit and the Son, was solved by separating them as two distinct divine "persons." The final outcome of Paul's equation of the Spirit and the Son was the doctrine of a Trinity of different persons. The church's early experience of a new and unique presence of the Spirit ironically matured into a theology that made the Spirit one aspect of the universal God pervading all creation.

Relating the Spirit and the Son, and preserving the divinity of the Spirit without submerging the uniqueness of the Spirit's presence in the Christian assemblies, continued to create problems long after the doctrine of the Trinity. The Eastern and Western churches split in part over the *filioque* clause in the Nicene creed, which says the Spirit proceeds from the Father *and the Son.* In its insistence on the *filioque* clause and the model of the Spirit coming through the Son, the Western church struggled to preserve Paul's identification of Jesus and the Spirit. Against the doctrine of the Trinity, with its separate "persons," the West stressed that what the Spirit primarily communicates is the Son. A hint of the subordination of the Spirit to Jesus continued in the West, along with the corresponding tendency to confine the Spirit to the church. In rejecting the *filioque* clause, the East drove the Spirit directly into the mystery of God himself and maintained the separate integrity of the life of the Spirit. The ancient idea of the Spirit as the universal divine wisdom was preserved in the East, but at the cost of an equal sense of the uniqueness of the Spirit in the church.

In two areas the witness of the early church was unclear: the relation of Jesus and the Spirit, and the relation of the Spirit and the church. On the relation of Jesus and the Spirit, three options developed from the early church's lack of clarity: (1) The classical Trinitarian formula *makes the Spirit relatively independent of the Son;* Thomas Aquinas comes as close as possible to this position in the West with his emphasis on the Spirit as the universal presence of God. (2) Traditional Western Trinitarianism has always tried to balance the independence of the Spirit by practically, if not theoretically, *subsuming the Spirit under the Son;* John Calvin gives some attention to the work of the Spirit throughout creation but implies that the primary work of the Spirit is to mediate the Son. (3) Friedrich Schleiermacher rejects any attempt to universalize the work of the Spirit; returning to one strand of New Testament teaching, he simply makes *the Spirit synonymous with the Son.* Three models can be schematized as follows: Aquinas, emphasizing the relative independence and cosmic work of the Spirit; Calvin subsuming the work of the Spirit under the work of Christ; Schleiermacher equating the work of the Spirit with the work of Jesus. (These men's positions are further elaborated in the following chapter.)

Following Aquinas in emphasizing the relative independence of the Spirit gives integrity to the Spirit's work. The Spirit not only continues the work of Christ, the Spirit is free to create the genuinely new. The gifts of the Spirit are not only extensions of Christ, they are a new stage in the salvation history. The Spirit creates a world of his own, he not only points to the past world of the Cross or a future Kingdom at the end. The present has value in itself. What goes on now, under the guidance of the Spirit, makes a positive contribution to the salvation of the world. Yet the uniquely Christian aspects of the Spirit can be lost here. The universal can triumph over the particular, as the abstract presence of God in all creation is given preference over the concrete revelation of God in the ministry of Jesus and the life of the church. The creative independence of the Spirit cannot be purchased at the price of the decisive knowledge of God in Jesus without the Spirit becoming vague or distorted. Torn loose from any grounding in Christ, there is nothing to keep the power of the Spirit from being identified with the power of blood and soil as the Nazis did or with the furthest flights of human imagination in Romanticism.

For Calvin, the present is decisively the age of the Spirit. Christ has died and risen and is waiting in the wings to come again; now is the time of the Spirit. But subsuming the Spirit under Christ tends to evacuate the present of meaning. The Spirit only points beyond himself to the Lord; he can only look backward to the Cross, upward to the ascended King, forward to the one who comes. He cannot witness to himself. While appearing to open the door to a new emphasis on the Spirit, Calvin firmly closes it by binding the Spirit so closely to the Son; the work of the Spirit and the church are only ancillaries to the work of redemption. As the master of balance, Calvin tries to harmonize this Christ-centered Spirit with the universal Spirit of Trinitarian orthodoxy. In doing so he attempts to do justice to the breadth of New Testament experience, which knows of both the universal presence of God and the unique communion with him brought by Christ. Concentrating on the universal presence of God makes it hard to understand why the particular Christ is important; focusing only on Jesus does not make clear his relation to the world he had a share in creating. Suggesting that the Spirit who unites the believer to Christ is the same Spirit that creates and sustains the world makes clear that there is an order and continuity in God's work. Creation, redemption, the ongoing work of the Spirit and the church in history are not random events. They must be understood in connection with one another; the fullness of God's plan is not found in any one of them taken by itself. This continuity and order is the appeal of Calvin's attempt to retain both the Spirit active in the world and the Spirit uniquely present in the church. Clarity about this order is lost by Calvin's inability to specify exactly how the Spirit binding us to Christ supplements, augments, or continues the work of energizing the Creation. Something of the drama and power of the Creation, the Cross, and the Spirit-filled church might be sacrificed by an exclusive concentration on their continuity and order.

Schleiermacher safeguards the uniqueness of the Christian life by deriving it wholly from Christ. If the Spirit is the only link between the believer and Christ, then (given the uniqueness and divinity of Christ), the uniqueness and divinity of Christian experience is preserved. Running throughout the New Testament is the early church's participation in the power and life of God in a radically new way. Making the Holy Spirit solely a gift from Christ serves (as it did for Schleiermacher) to break any facile connection between the Old Testament and the New and any evolutionary optimism about Christianity calmly developing out of its antecedents. Pentecost represents a new dispensation; lifted up by the very Spirit of God, the Christian church is no longer of the world in which it was born. For Schleiermacher the uniqueness of the Spirit is the uniqueness of Christ. This Christocentric view of the Spirit can tie the church to Christ to the exclusion of everything else. The Spirit is the agent that preserves the radical newness of the Gospel, but at the price of having any uniqueness of his own. The experience of the Spirit preserves the integrity of the church by binding it to Christ but, at the same time, tearing it loose from the world God created. If the Spirit only brings to the believer what Christ did in the past, the present is a static replay of what happened before. Awareness of the decisive turning point represented by Christ cannot be allowed to obscure the boldness and initiative of the Spirit without Christianity becoming lost in the past. If all the excitement of the Gospel belongs to the years A.D. 1–33, then Christianity can easily become a religious antiquarianism.

SPIRIT AS MEDIATOR

From the New Testament to the present the church struggles to understand the Spirit as mediator. What does the Spirit mediate? The universal presence of God? Jesus Christ? A little bit of both? Some have rejected the Spirit as mediator. Those for whom God himself is manifestly present in his Creation see no need for any mediator. For believers with Romantic inclinations, the Spirit is not so much a mediator in the sense of a "go-between" as simply the designation of the visible presence of God. Christians who feel they know Jesus directly have no need for a third person to relate them to Jesus. For Paul, Christians are "in

Christ" in an immediate way and so the Spirit is identified with the presence of Christ (2 Cor. 3:17) and Paul simply alternates between describing Christians as being "in Christ" and "in the Spirit" (cf. Rom. 8:1-2; Phil. 2:1). Schleiermacher, while denying access to the historical Jesus, insists that believers experience his influence directly, and so calls this influence by the title of Spirit. Here the Spirit is not a mediator but only a designation for the presence of Christ. Not needing the Spirit as mediator, Paul gives him other functions—through his gifts he builds up the community.

For Luke, the Ascension creates a break in the work of God, which shifts the focus from Jesus to the Spirit. Repeating the story of the Ascension twice (Luke 24:50ff; Acts 1:6-11), Luke emphasizes the departure of Jesus who "parted from them" and was "taken up . . . into heaven." His absence makes a place now for the coming Spirit. Thus Luke reiterates the need for the Spirit in telling the Ascension story: the Apostles must not leave Jerusalem until they are "clothed with power from on high" (Luke 24:49), and instead of answering the disciple's question about the time of his return, Jesus instructs them in the power of the Spirit (Acts 1:8). John, too, implies that the Spirit takes up where Jesus' historical ministry leaves off. The Spirit cannot come until the completion of Jesus' earthly role (John 7:39), and so the Lord tells his followers that "it is to your advantage that I go away, for if I do not leave, the Paraclete will not come" (John 16:7). For Luke and John the gulf between the disciples and Jesus caused by the close of his historical ministry produces a situation for the Spirit to be a mediator. This third party fills the vacuum created by the Lord's absence. The newly fallen Spirit provides the disciples with access to God and guides and directs them as

Jesus had done. This Spirit is a third reality and not simply another designation for Jesus. Aquinas and Calvin continue this tradition of the Spirit as mediator between Jesus and his followers.

The rise of historical criticism may give impetus in the modern world to recover this model of the Spirit as mediator. The language of mediator makes most sense in the context of a separation between Jesus and those who would be his disciples, and scholars are making the modern church aware of such a separation. In the nineteenth century, scientific historical inquiry addressed itself to the New Testament, brimming with confidence that its somewhat rationalistic and skeptical tools could untangle the authentic historical data in the Gospels from what the early church had added to enhance the picture of Jesus. Knowing in advance what could be authentic and what could not (ethical teaching was authentic, miracles were not), the nineteenth century produced many biographies of Jesus after its own image. Jesus was pictured as a perfect man of the nineteenth century—a son of the enlightenment and romantic ethos, a teacher of moral wisdom, and an example to men.

Historical method advanced and realized that the first rule of sound research was to see a figure in his own context. Jesus was now seen as a man of his own time: one who shared the beliefs of his age that the world would soon end and that mental illness is caused by demons. The new picture of Jesus as a fanatical prophet and miracle worker of the first century was no doubt more accurate, but it served up to nineteenth-century skeptical believers a figure alien and foreign to their own lives. What the early biographies of Jesus lacked in historical accuracy they made up for in religious relevance. The later scholars purchased historical accuracy about Jesus at the cost of a figure who can become the object of piety.

In various ways modern theology has tried to bridge the gap between the present believer and Jesus now locked in the past by historical criticism. There is demythologizing—letting go of the Jesus of past history in favor of the meaning of Christianity for each person's life. Or writing new lives of Jesus to make him a more compatible figure as a political revolutionary or the precursor of drug-expanded consciousness. Or focusing on a particular aspect of his existence and by implication relegating the rest to background importance, as Protestant evangelical theology does with the Cross, or liberal Christianity does with parts of his teaching.

When the early church felt that his Ascension caused a separation between their lives and their Lord, Pentecost provided the solution. As the modern church feels separated from Jesus after the failure of several "quests for the historical Jesus," which turned up either no Jesus at all or a Jesus with no religious importance, the present renewed interest in the Spirit of Pentecost may provide it with a solution. If Jesus is presently imprisoned in the past, the present remains the era of the Spirit. The hiddenness of Jesus may help regain a sense of the independence of the Spirit in churches that have always subsumed the Spirit under the Christ. As scholars puzzle over the historical Jesus, believers are rediscovering the third person of the Trinity as a mediator between God and man.

SPIRIT AND CHURCH

Inseparable from the dilemma of Jesus and the Spirit is the dilemma of the Spirit and the church. Those who tend to equate the Spirit and the Christ tend to limit the Spirit to the church as the Body of Christ. Those who see the Spirit as an independent manifestation of divinity tend to expand the work of the Spirit throughout the cosmos. Aquinas, by defining the Spirit as God's volition, implied that the Spirit is present everywhere, as God sustains and governs the universe by his will. Calvin bound the Spirit and Christ together and concentrated more on the special workings of the Spirit in the lives of Christians than on the cosmic work of the Spirit. Schleiermacher resolves the problem dogmatically by declaring that the New Testament teaches only the presence of the Spirit in the church; as the influence of Christ, the Spirit is only present with those sensitive to his life. Aquinas and Calvin are both caught between wanting to affirm the universal presence of the Spirit as demanded by the Trinitarian formula and to do justice to the special work of the Spirit in bringing people to Christ. Schleiermacher, in his dogmatics, defines the entire Godhead as immanent and doesn't need the Spirit to fill this role. Thus, he sees no problem in restricting the Spirit to the church.

Saying that the Spirit is active both universally and within the church emphasizes the continuity between the church and the world. The church can and must discern the Spirit working in the world on the basis of its exposure to the Spirit in the church, and the church can comprehend its experience of the Spirit in terms learned from the world of science, psychology, sociology, etc. Focusing on the spiritual bond between the church and the world means that the Spirit is driving the church out of itself into the world where the same Spirit is active. It means the church can understand itself on the model of other institutions in the world. If the Spirit that gave birth to the church has been working since Creation in all men, especially perhaps the children of Israel, then the origin of Christianity can be understood theologically as a process of historical development, and the continuity between Christianity and other religions, especially Judaism, can be maintained. Such openness of the church to the world implicit in the orthodox doctrine of the the Trinity, which universalizes the Spirit's work, comes at a loss of the New Testament tradition of special spiritual gifts to the church. Forcing the Spirit to function as the immanent and cosmic presence of God allowed the church to lose sight of the particular work of the Spirit in forming the Body of Christ into community. Gaining sensitivity to the world ought not to mean quenching the fire and killing the spiritual life of the church.

Concentrating on the uniqueness of the Spirit suddenly regains the dynamic of the early church: lives transformed, people cured, communities created before our eyes. In a time when the power of God seems to have evaporated from the midst of the churches, many call the church to regain her vitality by focusing all her attention on the special gifts God gives to his people. Coming to a sectarian equation of the Kingdom of the Spirit with the church, they exhort the denominations to leave the world alone and look inside themselves to the fire that burns in their hearts. Resurrection of the uniquely Christian work of the Spirit comes through the death of any continuity between the church and the world in terms of the doctrine of the Spirit.

The modern church is confronted with a problem, similar to that found in the early church, of the universalizing of the Spirit's work versus his uniqueness in the church. Secular theologies demand that the church abandon the claim to uniqueness and dissolve itself into the world; Pentecostals call on the church to abandon the world and fan the flames of its own Spirit. The church could universalize the doctrine of the Spirit and lose any hope of the genuine renewal which comes through the Spirit of Pentecost or concentrate on its special spiritual gifts and become a sect. But there are other options.

Abandoning a sense of continuity with the world through the Spirit need not mean theologically withdrawing from the world altogether. Concentrating on the unique gifts of the Spirit to the church still allows continuity with the world to be maintained in other ways. The Gospel of John implies that the Paraclete is a new gift given by Jesus only to his disciples, to keep them close to their Lord (John 14:16-17; 16:7; 12-15). In John, the Spirit seems subsumed under Jesus (16:13-15) and limited to the church (14:16-17). For John, the continuity between the church and creation is made not through the Spirit but through the Son. The Son (not the Spirit) is the light that enlightens every man; through the Word, not through the Spirit, was the world created (John 1:1-5). Seeing Christ in cosmic terms, as the one who embraces the universe, would free the church to attend to the unique gifts of the Spirit in her midst without losing sight of the world.

Building up the Body of Christ is the main function of the Spirit according to Paul (1 Cor. 12). The gifts of the Spirit are special endowments for the church to form Christian community (1 Cor. 12:7; 14:12; Eph. 4:11-12). Heavy concentration on these spiritual gifts and on Christian community does not overshadow concern for a cosmic work of the Spirit. The Spirit's goal is not the creation of charismatic sects but filling all things with the presence of God (Eph. 1:9-14). Special spiritual gifts and tightly organized Christian communities are not to forsake the world: God is creating them for the sake of the world. This means-ends model allows Paul to exhort the churches to exercise spiritual gifts and yet not lose sight of the entire creation. Working to build Christian community does not mean neglecting society, if it is only through such communities that society can be redeemed. Attending to the spiritual gifts does not mean despising the creation if, through the spiritual gifts, the creation will be filled with the presence of God. Paul's theology of the plan of God as the filling of the cosmos with the Spirit through Christian community and spiritual gifts would enable the church to become resensitized to the unique and powerful works of the Spirit in the body of Christ without losing touch with its responsibility for the world for which Christ died.

Modern Pentecostals are an exception to the doctrinal lines here laid down. Generally, those maintaining the relative independence of the Spirit identify the Spirit with the immanence of God and universalize the Spirit's presence. Pentecostals emphasize the autonomy of the Spirit. The Pentecostal dispensation is radically new; the gifts of the Spirit are signs of a new age, not of anything that has happened before. The Spirit does not simply enliven what Christ did, the Spirit creates a new reality of new languages, tongues of fire, communities of love. Yet they concentrate on the particular aspects of Christianity and not its cosmic dimensions. Often they are sectarians who withdraw from the world; even those who aren't sectarian often implicitly limit the important work of the Spirit to the Christian church.

The relative freedom and spontaneity of the Spirit is maintained by the Pentecostals' insistence on the independence of the Spirit; however, since the Spirit is not identified with the divine immanence but with a Divine

Person who lives with the Christian community, the independence of the Spirit need not be traded off against the importance of the church as it has been in so much Western theology. The Pentecostals' inchoate theology retains the independence of the Spirit while concentrating on the Spirit in the church. Such a theology is important as the modern church seeks to renew itself through a recovery of the power of the Spirit and of Christian community.

The weakness of the Pentecostals' theology is its bordering on sectarianism. Can the church adapt this theology and regain its unique possession of the Spirit and its koinonia without losing its openness to the world? The New Testament offers a tentative yes. John locates the universality of Christianity in the Word made flesh, not the Spirit poured out on the church. Paul rejects sectarianism and keeps his eyes on the whole cosmos by seeing the Spirit working through the particular community for the sake of the universal plan of God. The church has traditionally maintained the universality of the Gospel through the doctrine of the Spirit by calling the Spirit the immanence of God. This world-embracing openness has come at the cost of openness to the particular and powerful work of the Spirit in Christian community. Conversely, those sects that have regained the power of the Spirit in the church have usually lost the cosmic sense of the Gospel. Sacrificing the universality traditionally provided by the doctrine of the Spirit may not be too great a price for the modern church to pay for a renewal of the Pentecostal power in her midst, especially if the universal reach of the Gospel can be maintained through the logos theology of John or the cosmic theology of Paul. In this way the modern American church can fulfill the responsibility to renew itself by incorporating the charismatic Spirit in its heart without losing its mission to the world.

In one dramatic way the New Testament understanding of the Spirit eludes the modern church. In the New Testament the manifestations of the Spirit are public demonstrations of the Spirit's power. When Luke speaks of receiving the Spirit he does not mention any rush of feelings but rather preaching with power, speaking unknown languages, witnessing to Jesus (Acts 4:31-33; 10:44-46; 19:6). For Paul the gifts of the Spirit are readily visible abilities to lead the community, to heal, to prophecy (1 Cor. 12:4-12; Eph. 4:11-12). According to Calvin and Aquinas the Spirit manifests himself outwardly in moral action, the confession of faith, the corporate life of the church.

Calvin, however, lays increasing stress on such inward works of the Spirit as "illumination" and "sealing the heart." These are the workings of the transcendent God, but the work of the Spirit appears subjective in that, to a greater extent than in the New Testament, the basic manifestations of the Spirit are internal. Creating faith is the primary work of the Spirit for Calvin and it has two stages: illuminating the mind and enlivening the heart. The object of faith is the Word of God and so the Spirit's work is objective in that it is directed at something outside of the individual's private world, but it remains subjective in that the manifestations of the Spirit are wholly internal to the self. Certainty, which is the most important part of faith for

Calvin, is based on an inward response of the heart. "It remains to pour into the heart itself what the mind has absorbed," Calvin writes, "for the Word of God is not received by faith . . . [until] it takes root in the depth of the heart."

Schleiermacher set the modern temperament by totally subjectivizing the Spirit. Rejecting the idea that the Spirit influences man from outside, Schleiermacher says that the Spirit is "determined from within and only this . . . is the sphere of the Holy Spirit." Seeing the Spirit as a personal influence beyond human consciousness is too close to the primitive imagery of the Old Testament. The Spirit is wholly immanent within man and is entirely "bound up" with human nature. The Spirit is a name for the potential for religious experience within each person, which is awakened through contact with the influence of Jesus in the church. In restricting the Spirit to the inner life, Schleiermacher set the tone for most modern theology.

The subjectivizing of the Holy Spirit parallels what might be called the major problem in contemporary theology—the crisis of theological authority. For Aquinas, the church, supported by the scriptures and reason, was the authority for the Christian. In the breakdown of the authority of the church during the Reformation, Calvin seized on the Scripture as the solution to the crisis of authority in his day. The authoritativeness of the Bible, for Calvin, lay in its being confirmed by the Spirit in the heart and mind of the believer. The same Spirit who inspired the Bible writers inspires the Bible readers that it is true. The Book itself is not an authority, it is confirmed as an authority by the Spirit's inner testimony. The grounds of faith are both objective and subjective: objective in that

God's Word stands beyond man's private world, subjective in that its authority is not complete until it is confirmed within man's heart and mind. Theological authority is contained in this dialectic of objectivity and subjectivity, the outer Word and the inner Spirit, the transcendent power of God manifest in an interior human experience.

The Reformation created the crisis of authority in Calvin's time by undercutting the authority of the church; the rise of historical criticism created the crisis of authority for Schleiermacher by calling into question the historicity of the Bible. Affected by historical skepticism, Schleiermacher could not accept the Bible as authoritative in the way Calvin did, and so there remained to him out of Calvin's dialectic only the subjective element. Taking the written word away from the Calvinist balance of the Word and the inner experience left Schleiermacher with only inward experience as the basis for religious authority.

This did not lead immediately to as radical a subjectivizing of religious authority as one might have suspected. Schleiermacher retained something of Calvin's dialectic of objectivity and subjectivity, although he truncated it in a more subjective direction. The Spirit, as the corporate ethos of the church, possesses a certain objectivity; the community might serve as a check on the feelings of its members. Since, for Schleiermacher, the manifestations of the Spirit are totally interior, there is no possibility of public confirmation of them by the community. Thus the community can't really function as an authority for Schleiermacher although, since the Spirit belongs both to the church and to its members, the church might insure some objectivity to the Spirit's work.

Thus the problem passes to the present. Freud is probably

most responsible for the crisis of theological authority in our day. Aquinas thought faith could be supported by an infallible church, but the reformers convinced many that the church can and did err. Calvin thought he could base his faith on an infallible Bible, but historical criticism convinced many that the Bible, too, could be wrong. Schleiermacher assumed that man's private world was secure from any scientific attack and that faith could be grounded on feelings. Freud dissolved these feelings into a cauldron of neurosis and convinced many that religious experience is only neurotic projection and unconscious wish-fulfillment. The church, the Bible, religious experience have all been cut down, and modern theology flounders without a foundation.

A new sensitivity to the Spirit will rebuild the theological foundations in our day. If meaning can be given to the objectivity of the Spirit's work, then the experience of the Spirit in the charismatic movement can lead the church out of this crisis of authority. A first step might be to recover the dialectic of Word and Spirit as a balance where both receive equal weight. Traditionally few Christian groups have maintained this balance intact. Some have subtly placed the Word over the Spirit and subsumed the Spirit under the Scripture, until the only function of the Spirit is to witness to the Bible. The Reformed scholasticism of the seventeenth century and the fundamentalist literalists in America, descended from the Princeton Theology of Hodge and Warfield, are examples of this. Those sectarians who place the Spirit above and beyond the Bible undo the balance from the other side.

Giving equal authority to the Bible and the Spirit means that the Book itself has no meaning apart from the Spirit. If the Bible were "objective" in the way that American

Protestant literalism teaches—that it needs no confirmation outside of its own text—then an atheist ought to be converted simply on reading the words. Calvin was more realistic in saying, "Without the illumination of the Holy Spirit, the Word can do nothing." Luther identified the text of the Scripture with the law, which brought only death; the Word of God is the "inner word" revealed by the Spirit. Calvin and Luther emphasize that the letter of the Bible is of little value without the sovereign work of the Spirit.[1] The Bible has no significance when ripped from the context of the experience of the Spirit. Refusing to subsume the Spirit under the Word frees the Spirit to do more than simply confirm the text and then shut up. The word *Paraclete* means not only a comforter but also a guide who "will lead you into all truth." The Spirit is as much a guide to the Christian as the Bible. The Spirit does not contradict the Scriptures but his job is more than just repeating what one can find by reading there. At the end of the Gospel, John indicates that the Lord expected the Spirit to direct the church in those many areas not covered by Jesus' teachings (John 15:7-12). The Book of Acts makes it clear that, just as the miracles of the Spirit are to take their place alongside the preaching of the Gospel as signs for those outside (Acts 4:29-30; cf. Romans 15:18-19; 1 Cor. 2:4-5), so the experience of the Spirit is equal with the testimony of the Scriptures as an authority for those inside. Confronting the problem of how much of the Jewish law the Gentiles should obey, the first apostolic council went back to the Old Testament covenant with Noah but justified their decision by saying "it seemed good to the Holy Spirit and to us" (Acts 15:28; 11:15-17). In giving instruction to new churches, St. Paul supports himself with Old Testament texts, but sometimes it is enough authority for him if he can say, "In this I have the Spirit of the Lord" (e.g., 1 Cor. 7:40).

Giving equal authority to the experiences of the Spirit and the text of the Bible is only half the story. Rebuilding the full foundations of the Christian religion also means recovering the Pauline emphasis on the Spirit in community. The polemics of the past have separated the Bible from the Spirit in the community, and therefore destroyed any valid basis for Christian faith. Protestants have the Bible, but the Bible without the Spirit and the community is a dead letter giving rise to arid scholasticism. Catholics have the community, but the community without the Bible and the Spirit becomes only an institutional shell. Pentecostals have the Spirit but the Spirit without the Bible and the community inevitably leads to subjectivism and fanaticism. This sundering of the three authorities has relegated Christianity to the realm of subjectivity. A charismatic ecumenism that drew together the community, the Word, and the Spirit would point a way out of the impasse created by the modern antithesis of objectivity and subjectivity and restore a measure of objectivity to religion.

What do we mean by objectivity? Ordinarily we take all of our experience pretty much for granted; we assume that when we experience something it is *really* there in some sense. We don't ordinarily question our experience unless it starts to get us into trouble. The most common way our experience gets us into trouble is when it contradicts someone else's experience. If I say that it's really hot in this room and someone else says it's quite chilly, then I have to stop and think. Before my experience was contradicted, I assumed that I was sensing the temperature correctly. Now I may wonder if I have a fever or am dressed too heavily. What happens when our experience is contradicted? How do we determine if our experience is giving us a correct or objective account of the world? We resort to something I'll term "communal verification."

Supposing I walk into my classroom and see a pink elephant sitting in the corner. Since this is not an ordinary occurrence I want to find out if the creature is really there. I ask my students if they, too, see a pink elephant. If they all say yes, I have pretty good warrant for assuming that, for some strange reason, there *is* a pink elephant there (unless I have reason to believe someone is playing a trick on all of us). If they all say no, I will begin to suspect I am having an illusion; at least I would have little warrant for saying that there was a pink elephant there. If I did, the students could rightly respond that my assertion of the existence of a pink elephant was mere subjectivity.

By objectivity we simply mean communal verification; objective assertions are those for which we have some support from other's experience. Subjectivity is simply the absence of such communal support; we call an assertion subjective when it seems to refer only to our own experience. I am not saying that only objective assertions are true in some sense. Fifty million Frenchmen can be wrong, and there might be a pink elephant in my office that only I can see. I'm not talking about what is true in the ordinary meaning of the word. I'm doing something much more modest and only discussing what we mean by the terms objective and subjective and when we can legitimately say that something is objective. A statement can be called objective if it has some communal verification; the extent of its support in the experience of others is the extent of its objectivity.

This apparent digression into the definition of words does not solve all our problems, but it may clarify some of them and it has some interesting implications for the subject at hand. The best illustration of this principle is from the field of knowledge regarded as most objective by our society, the natural sciences. Many modern writers on the philosophy of science point out that science, too, proceeds by communal verification. Perhaps the most extensive and persuasive proponent of this thesis is Michael Polanyi who argues for it at length in his book *Personal Knowledge*.[2] The scientist relies not only on his perception of the data but also checks them against the perception of others. And not just anybody's perceptions count; the perceptions and ideas of similarly trained scientists weigh most heavily. Science is not only a function of the way the world is, it is also a function of the way in which *the community of scientists* perceives the world to be. There is no way to stand outside that community and check to see if their perceptions are really true, because the criteria for what is really true in science is determined by this community.

What happens when communal verification breaks down? Supposing, when I ask my class about the pink elephant, exactly half say they see it and half say they don't. For every two people who enter the room, one says yes and one votes no. How, then, can I tell if the elephant is really there? The same problems occur in science. The results of experiments commissioned by the American Psychological Association and done under the most rigorous of standards, which seem to demonstrate the existence of some form of extrasensory perception, are so statistically significant that, in any other field, they would be regarded as almost conclusive. Yet most psychologists refuse to accept the results because they contradict all the known theoretical frameworks in which psychology works. Some scientists on the far fringes of subatomic physics feel it necessary to posit certain entities to make their theories consistent, which other physicists do not find need for. Simply appealing to evidence will not solve these kinds of disputes because either (1) the two groups are disagreeing about the fundamental question of what counts for evidence or (2) they agree on the facts but it's the interpretation of them by each group that cannot be resolved.

Claims to objectivity, then, are relative to certain communities; a claim that something is known objectively is the claim that it is known within the terms of some community. If I wonder whether my experience is giving me objective knowledge, I check it against the experience of others; if my experience is of a particularly sophisticated sort (like that of subatomic physicists) I must check it within a very limited and sophisticated community. Emphasizing that the Christian's experience of the Spirit takes place within a community is to make the same point in different terms. If the balance between Word and Spirit also demands a balance between Word, Spirit, and community then Christianity retains its communal verification. Understanding the Bible and the workings of the Spirit take place within a community and are verified (or falsified) by that community in a way analogous to the experience of a physicist taking place within and being verified by the community of physicists. When a Christian can recognize in his own experience of the Spirit close parallels to what is described in the New Testament, to what the saints throughout the history of the church have taught, and to what other members of his community are also experiencing, there is no reason for him to let his experience be called merely subjective. It has received a measure of communal verification. It is not simply a function of his own private subjectivity.

Christian experience is decisively community-relative; but that is true of all our knowledge. We have no claims to knowledge about anything in this world or the next apart from communities that give us the terms in which we think and that validate our experiences as more than private illusions. We may judge the experiences of one community by another (say evaluating religion in the terms of psychology) but that is not escaping communal verification, it is just substituting one community of experience, which we happen to prefer, for another. One may get a greater degree of communal verification for some kinds of experiences than for others; but all deeply significant or highly sophisticated experiences are verified within relatively small groups. Ordinary experiences of trees, tables, and chairs are supported quite readily. But these are not particularly significant. Intense artistic creativity, complex theoretical work in science, potent religious experiences are all supported within much smaller communities. What happens when communities disagree—as when psychologists, sociologists, philosophers, and theologians disagree about the nature of religion, or when two religious communities see things differently? Well, that's like what happens when 50 percent of the people see the pink elephant and 50 percent do not.[3]

Beside restoring a certain wholeness to the foundations of Christianity, shattered by the separation of the community, the Bible, and the Spirit, balancing Scripture and Spirit and seeing community as the locus of the Spirit opens new directions for understanding the relation of the Bible and the church. Protestants have tended to picture the Bible as an inerrant authority standing atop the community, Catholics often picture the church sitting in judgment on the Scriptures. Linked by the Spirit, who inspires and validates the Scriptures and also creates the community, Bible and church fall into place together. The Bible is written by and for the church. Inspired by the Spirit who builds up the Body and written by members of the church seeking to serve it, the Bible cannot be understood when ripped out of context. In the ethos of a community formed by the Spirit, the Bible is read with understanding. Through their participation in charismatic communities, Catholics and Protestants from traditions not particularly Bible-oriented are finding the Scripture takes on new meaning. In the same way, many Pentecostals traditionally strong on the Bible are finding that the New Testament speaks to them of the church. The charismatic movement is full of stories of Christians from very individualistic backgrounds forming together into community. These are the practical results of a theological shift toward restoring the balance between the Bible and the community and away from a Bible standing over a church or a church sitting on top of its Scriptures.

In recovering the integrity of Christian experience by reuniting Bible, Spirit, and church, a new theology of the Spirit, built around community, opens up new ecumenical directions. The point of the ecumenical movement is not to unite empty bureaucracies but to restore the foundations of Christianity. A theology of the Spirit in community preserves the Catholic, Protestant, and sectarian-Pentecostal influences by harmonizing the authority of the Bible, the community, and the spiritual experience of the believer. Catholicism has emphasized the church; Protestantism the Bible; liberalism and Pentecostalism the experience of the believer. In a theology that saw the foundation of Christianity as a balance of Word and Spirit in the context of community, these three poles of Christian theology and Christian life are not sundered or set in opposition but are laid open to the possibility of creative harmony. In the complete Spirit-filled body of Christ, as Paul portrays it, these three partial authorities complement each other. The Spirit inspires the Word and builds up the community; the Word enables us to understand our experience of the Spirit and teaches us the form of our common life; the community forms the context in which the Word is understood and the Spirit encountered. Using the Bible to tear down rather than build up the church, using the church to squelch the Spirit, using the Spirit as a pretext to go beyond the perimeters of the Gospel have destroyed the foundations of Christianity in the modern world more than any external attacks by atheists and skeptics. In their experience of the Spirit in community, many Catholics, Protestants, and Pentecostals are experiencing the restoring of these foundations as they see the Bible, the Spirit, and the community live together and build each other up as parts of the one body of Christ.

4

Historical Supplement

Acknowledging that those who ignore history are doomed to repeat it, any constructive theology of the Holy Spirit today ought to draw on the ideas of past theologians. Certain perennial problems occur in any discussion of the Third Person of the Trinity—his relation to Christ, the church, the world—and knowledge of how others have wrestled with them gives the modern thinker new ideas and enlarged perspectives. Also, every Christian inherits certain concepts and formulas. This inheritance is the context in which Christian theology takes place, no matter how much that heritage is altered or rejected. Knowing the origin and background of the puzzles about the Spirit and the terms used to discuss them provides the contemporary theologian with insight into them. This final chapter is really supplementary; the constructive task of the book was completed in chapter 3. This material buttresses what was said before by providing the story of the doctrine of the Spirit in the early church and an analysis of three men who represent different eras and approaches to the Spirit.

PROBLEMS AND PREMONITIONS: THE EARLY CHURCH

Attempts to comprehend the Holy Spirit began as soon as the primitive church was born out of the Pentecostal encounter with the Spirit. From the beginning Christians not only experienced the Spirit but reflected on their experience. This reflection did not take place in a vacuum but in a context formed primarily by the life of the children of Israel. Hebrew religious life did not cease growing in the fifth century B.C. with Ezra's restoration of Judaism to the land of Israel. Rather it evolved and multiplied into many different branches during the period from the Restoration to the beginning of the Christian church. All of these branches had common roots in the law and the Prophets, but all grew at a slightly different angle from the trunk.

Two of these branches were particularly influential in forming the context in which the early church reflected on its experience of the Spirit. One of these was the tradition of Jewish wisdom, which can be found in the intertestamental books of the Wisdom of Solomon and The Wisdom of Jesus ben Sirach. The Hebrew wise men refined the teachings of the fathers into short sayings of practical benefit, such as those found in the book of Proverbs. In doing so, they claimed to be guided by God's spirit, which they called wisdom. The other branch was the apocalyptic tradition, which combined the ancient Israelite faith in God's power to intervene in history with the oppressive circumstances in which the intertestamental Jew found himself to produce a fervent hope in that final day when God would act decisively and Israel would be vindicated. These two traditions were not contradictory. They may have touched each other before the Christian era. But they did come together in a new way when they merged with the Pentecostal experience of the early church.

The wisdom tradition of the intertestamental period personified wisdom itself as the mediator between man and God. As a good mediator must, wisdom was divine enough to be able to reveal God. Yet she was not so far removed from man as to be inaccessible to him. Man's mind was formed by wisdom and so could embrace her in its reach. Man's mind did not create wisdom; she came from God. She was called the breath of God and the emanation of his glory (Wisd. of Sol. 7:25). She was with God from the beginning of his creation, having been created before the cosmos (Prov. 8:22-31). The wise men called her *pneuma* (spirit) and *charism* (gift) (Wisd. of Sol. 1:6; 8:21; 7:27). But she not only came from God. Being the ground of man's own reason, she was implanted in his being, too, and was thereby able to mediate God and man.

The wise men of Israel, although preoccupied with the cosmic significance of *Sophia* (the Greek name for wisdom), had not lost touch with the faith of their fathers in a God who acted in their history. They gave wisdom a central place in the holy history of their people. It was wisdom, they said, that brought the Sons of Israel out of Egypt (Wisd. of Sol. 10:18-21). It was wisdom that inspired the Patriarchs (Wisd. of Sol. 10:1-4; Wisd. of Jes. ben Sir. 4-45). It was the voice of Sophia that spoke through the prophets (Wisd. of Sol. 7:27).

It was not, however, the wise men who most jealously preserved the Hebrew heritage of a God who worked out his purposes in man's own history. Those Jews who looked past the rise and fall of the Greek and Roman empires to the day when God's triumph and his righteous Messiah would inaugurate his Kingdom shared their forefathers' faith in the mighty acts of God. They searched the Scriptures for a timetable of the last days. One of the passages they seized on, apparently, was the prophecy of Joel that in the last days God would pour out his Spirit on all flesh. Many signs and wonders would follow but the giving of the Spirit itself would be one of the major signs of the end of time.

The primitive church's reflection about the Spirit, as it appears in the New Testament, does not separate these two motifs (wisdom and eschatology). The dialectic between them forms the New Testament and the patristic understanding of the Spirit. These two traditions, while sharing much, were not in total agreement. They both provide categories in which the Spirit is discussed, but in so doing differences between them appear. To view the Spirit as a sign of the end does not necessarily imply that the Spirit is divine. In order for the Spirit to be identified with the categories of the wisdom mediator, he must be a divine being. And therein, so to speak, hangs the tale.

The book of Acts begins with the prophecy of Joel and the statement that the Spirit has been given as a fulfillment of the promise of a sign in the last days. This eschatological emphasis does not isolate Acts from the wisdom tradition, which speaks of wisdom being "poured out" and as a gift (Jes. ben Sir. 1:9-10; Wisd. of Sol. 8:21), the same terms Acts uses for the Spirit. But nothing in Acts necessarily entails that the Spirit be a divine being. The only place where Luke suggests that the Spirit is a divine being or wisdom mediator is when he writes "the Holy Spirit said 'separate to me Barnabas and Saul.' " Behind this may stand the connection between the Spirit and prophecy in the wisdom tradition.[1] The wisdom tradition linked together prophecy and the ability to discern God's will through wisdom. Thus Luke writes in his Gospel, "Therefore the sophia of God said, 'I will send to them prophets.' " Both the language of the wisdom tradition and the image of the Spirit as an eschatological sign can be found in Luke.

For Paul, too, the Spirit is closely tied with eschatology. For Paul, the expectation of the end of history is of critical importance.[2] The Spirit is seen as the first fruits of the coming Kingdom; it is a down payment on the future (1 Cor. 5:5; 1:22). But the Spirit is more, for Paul, than an eschatological sign. Paul draws on images similar to those of the wisdom tradition to give the Spirit a mediatorial role in the plan of God. The Wisdom of Solomon speaks of wisdom mediating to man the secrets of God, which man himself cannot discover. It is wisdom that knows the counsels of the Almighty and discerns the will of God. Paul writes that it is the Spirit that mediates the secrets of God to man. "God has revealed himself through the Spirit," Paul writes to the Corinthians (1 Cor. 2:10), echoing exactly what others had said of Sophia. "It is the Spirit that searches everything, even the depths of God," Paul goes on to say, in the same vein as the books that picture wisdom as dwelling in the divine depth. In the Wisdom of Solomon, Sophia is the source of goodness. Paul calls the virtues of the Christian life fruits of the Spirit.

In brief, the Wisdom of Solomon says:

> In her [wisdom] there is a spirit that is intelligent, holy, unique, manifold, subtle, mobile, clear, unpolluted, distinct, invulnerable, loving the good, keen, irresistible, beneficent, humane, steadfast, sure, free from anxiety, all-powerful, overseeing all, and penetrating through all spirits that are intelligent and pure and most subtle. For wisdom is more mobile than any motion; because of her pureness she pervades and penetrates all things. For she is a breath of the power of God and a pure emanation of the glory of the Almighty. . . . She is a reflection of eternal light, a

spotless mirror of the working of God, and an image of his goodness. Though she is but one, she can do all things, and while remaining in herself, she renews all things. In every generation she passes into holy souls and makes them friends of God and prophets (7:22–27).

This might serve as a summary of the teaching of Paul about the Holy Spirit who "searches the hearts of men" and sanctifies them (Rom. 8:27; 15:16).

It has been suggested by some scholars that the Spirit was used by John, and perhaps Luke, to deal with the delay in the Second Coming of Christ.[3] The early church expected an imminent return of Christ, and the delay of this event created a crisis of faith, which, these scholars say, caused her to shift emphasis from the future coming of Christ to the present experience of the Spirit. However, in both Luke and John, the Spirit is not connected with the gap between the church's expectation and the lack of the Second Coming, but with the gap between men and the ascended Christ. It is the Ascension and not the delay of the end that creates the need for the Spirit (Luke 21:49; Acts 1:8; cf. John 7:39; 16:7). For Luke, since Christ has ascended, he has gone beyond the range of men (Luke 24:5; Acts 1:9–11). In Acts, to be a Christian is not to know Christ directly but to believe the work which God did in Christ (Acts 2:22–38) and to receive the gift of the Spirit.

The exception to this is Paul, who identified his experience of the risen Christ with the post-Resurrection and pre-Ascension experiences of the disciples. Thus, Paul's description of his experience appears to "undo" the Ascension. Paul stands in another tradition from Luke at this point. For Paul, the Christian is not only one who believes in God's work through Jesus and has received the Spirit but is also one who is "in Christ" (Rom 8:1-2; Phil. 2:1). For Paul, then, the need for a mediator between the ascended Lord and man is undermined, since man can know directly the ascended Lord. So the difference between the Spirit and the Son becomes blurred. It is this blurring of roles that is passed on to the fathers of the early church.

New Testament churches sought to understand the Spirit by an interplay of the motifs of wisdom mediator and eschatological sign. Problems arose in the second century because the same wisdom categories that were applied to the Spirit also were applied to the Son. The use of the same images and the blurring of functions of both the Spirit and the Son meant that, as the use of the eschatological categories for the Spirit decreased, it became increasingly hard to distinguish the Spirit from the Son, for both were assigned the function of wisdom mediator. Beside making a distinction between the Son and the Spirit difficult, the New Testament imagery increasingly forced the developing church to see the Spirit as a Divine Person like the Son. The Spirit, too, took on the characteristics of the wisdom mediator—a Divine Being between God and man.

Justin Martyr, the first of the fathers to really discuss the Spirit, illustrates the continuing dependence of the doctrine of the Spirit upon the wisdom tradition and the confusion resulting from the identification of the Spirit and the Son with the same wisdom mediator. Justin was a Christian convert who had, apparently, been a teacher of philosophy before his conversion. After becoming a Christian, he continued as a teacher, expounding the doctrines of Christianity to the learned of his day. He was also a prolific writer. He lived in Rome and there was martyred for his faith. As a former student of Greek philosophy, he was familiar with the term "Logos," the Greek word referring to the cosmic order or Spirit, which pervades and governs the universe. A common term in Greek philosophy, it occurs often in the beginning of the Gospel of John, where it is usually translated "Word." It is clear that the function of the Logos in Greek philosophy is similar to that of Sophia in the Hebrew wisdom literature. Thus it was easy to combine the Greek Logos philosophy with the Hebrew wisdom tradition that had been taken over in Christian theology.

In his writings, Justin identifies the Logos, which had been equated with Jesus Christ, in the Gospel of John, with the Spirit, thus fusing both Son and Spirit. He was not the first to do this. Paul had said, "The Lord is the Spirit" (2 Cor. 3:17). The first-century letter of Ignatius says that Christians have "obtained the inseparable Spirit who is Jesus Christ."[4] The early Christian sermon, which has come down to us as "The *Shepard of Hermas*," says that the Incarnation was an incarnation of the Holy Spirit, which would unite the Spirit, the Logos, and Christ.[5] A second-century Christian sermon, called the "Second Epistle of Clement to the Corinthians," also says that Christ was the Spirit before he became Incarnate (9:5).[6]

Even more explicitly, Justin writes,

> It is wrong, therefore, to understand the Spirit and the power of God as anything else than the Word [Logos] who is also the first born of God, as the foresaid Moses declared; and it was this which, when it came upon the virgin and overshadowed her, caused her to conceive, not by intercourse but by power. And that all the prophets are inspired by no other than the Divine Word [Logos].[7]

Justin often reiterates that it was the divine Logos who spoke through the prophets. Attributing to the Logos (which was identified with the Son) the Spirit's traditional functions was the logical conclusion of the identification of both with the wisdom mediator and of Paul's statement that the Holy Spirit is the Spirit of the Son. After the eschatological motif drops out (none of the fathers speak of the Spirit as an eschatological sign), the only way remaining to speak of the Spirit was in terms of the motif of wisdom mediator. The images of wisdom were similar to the language about the Logos, already applied to the Son.

The importance of Justin's identification of Spirit and Son for the development of the church's understanding of the Spirit is impossible to overestimate. Now the outcome of the disputes concerning the Son were also to apply to the Spirit. After Justin, to call the Son divine was to entail the Spirit's divinity, too. The Son and the Spirit were linked in subsequent history, because the same tradition that explained the Spirit's role made him a Divine Being like the Son. As the stress increasingly fell on the mediatorial aspects of the Spirit's work and less on his function as a sign of the end, the issue of his divinity and his place in the Godhead was bound to be raised. This question of the Spirit's origin could be raised very easily following Justin's identification of the Spirit with the Logos. Now, to raise the issue of the divinity of the Logos–Son was also to raise the issue of the divinity of the Spirit, for the same terms applied to both.

This clearly can be seen in a theologian who was a follower of Justin, Irenaeus who was Bishop of Gaul in the second century. Irenaeus clearly affirms that the origin of the Spirit in the Godhead is the same as the origin of the Son. He writes, "I have also largely demonstrated that the Word, namely the Son, was always with the Father; and that Wisdom also, which is the Spirit, was present with him anterior to call creation."[8] Note the identification of the Spirit with wisdom. Having identified their origins, Irenaeus is free to confuse their functions. He says at one point it is the Spirit and at another point it is the Son who spoke through the prophets.

The terms wisdom and Logos imply that the Spirit is at work in all creation, for both Sophia and Logos refer to the order of the universe. But Irenaeus also goes back to a tradition mirrored in the book of Acts, which implies that the Spirit is a gift given especially to the church.[9] Christ, Irenaeus writes, confers the Spirit "upon those who are partakers of Himself."[10] Shorn of all eschatological significance, the stress falls on works of the Spirit done, not as signs of the last days, but as a validation of the Gospel in the present days. Irenaeus puts great apologetic emphasis on the value of the works of the Spirit done in his own day. He mentions the casting out of demons, the healing of the sick, and even resurrections from the dead, as signs done in his own time to validate the Gospel.

A detailed history of the subsequent controversy over the generation of the Logos and, by implication, the origin of the Spirit is not necessary here. This controversy, which ran throughout the third and fourth centuries, produced, in A.D. 381 at Constantinople, the orthodox doctrine of the Trinity as embodied in the Nicene Creed, with its affirmation of the full divinity of the Spirit. This controversy arose in the context of a dualistic view of reality, which separated reality into created (called "generate") and uncreated (called "ungenerate") existence. Justin identifies the Son and the Spirit with the Logos, which he calls generate, and the controversy is off and running. In the philosophy of his day, this would entail that the Logos could not be fully divine since only the uncreated reality is divine. But the developing doctrine of the church said that the Son and now by implication the Spirit are fully divine. Irenaeus tries to get around this by suggesting that the

Logos is "eternally created." This still makes the Logos created; and Irenaeus adds to the problem by suggesting that created existence is, by definition, imperfect and therefore not divine.

It fell to Origen to see this problem clearly. Origen was from Alexandria and was probably the most brilliant theologian of the Patristic period, although he was later condemned for heresy. Because he was more astute than his predecessors, he saw the implications of what they had said. Origen redefined the basic issue as one of change rather than generation. The Logos, he said, is eternally generate (or created) and is therefore changeless, since it is eternal. Thus it is akin to the divine, which is also unchangeable. Origen thought he had solved the problem. The Logos was still generate but it was also divine since it had the essential divine attribute of changelessness.

But then Methodius, a follower of Origen, introduced the notion of time into this scheme of Origen's.[11] This meant, once and for all, that if the Logos was created it could not be fully divine. By making creation something that occurs temporally, Methodius undermined Origen's idea of eternal creation. Therefore, there must have been a time when the Logos was not yet created. This became the slogan of Arius, who was a heretic who denied the full divinity of the Logos by saying it was a created and therefore subordinate being.

To combat the Arians, three theologians from the province of Cappadocia in Asia Minor redid the whole scheme. The Cappadocian fathers substituted a distinction between the essence (which they called "ousia") of something and the form in which it exists (which they called "hypostasis") for the distinction between the created and the uncreated. In philosophical terms, they removed the issue from the realm of cosmology and put it in the realm of ontology. Now the distinguishing feature of the Godhead was not its uncreatedness but its divine essence. This move meant that the Logos need no longer be conceived of in a philosophically contradictory way. The Logos was no longer the eternal but the created Son of the Father. Now the Son was, like the Father, a manifestation (hypostasis) of the one divine essence (ousia). Since the Spirit had been carried along with the Logos–Son in the mainstream of Christian theology since the time of Justin, it was inevitable that the Spirit, too, should become a hypostasis of the divine essence. The use of the category of essence to define the Godhead meant a radical break existed between the divine and the mundane realms. There could be no halfway beings like the Arian Logos—part divine, part created. The Spirit, too, had to be fully a part of the Godhead if he was to be at all divine. The only way to bring him into the Godhead was to make him a third hypostasis. Thus the classical doctrine of the Trinity took shape.

This whole line of development is summarized in Gregory of Nyssa's (one of the Cappadocian fathers) definitive treatise, "On the Holy Spirit." He wrote this to refute the Macedonians, a group who taught that the Son was equal with the Father, but that the Spirit was distinct from and subordinate to them. The existence of this group indicates that the tradition running from Paul through Justin and Irenaeus to the Cappadocians, which identified the Son and the Spirit, was not universally shared in the early church. One might say the Macedonians stopped the development of their thought about the Spirit at some point prior to full identification of the Spirit with the Logos. On the basis on the orthodox development, Gregory says to the Macedonians that if they admit the divinity of the Son they must also admit the divinity of the Spirit, since they belong together "according to the Scripture" and the tradition of the church. If the Spirit is divine, Gregory goes on, then he must be a divine hypostasis. Gregory therefore concludes "the Holy Spirit is of the same rank as the Father and the Son, so there is no difference between them in anything to be thought or named that devotion can describe to a divine nature."[12]

It was this formulation that became orthodox at the Council of Constantinople. The Spirit was, along with the Father and Son, a hypostasis of the divine ousia (or three persons in one divine substance, to use the Latin terms more familiar in the West). It was this definition of the Spirit in terms of ontology rather than eschatology or soteriology to which later generations were heir.

The major problem in the Patristic period concerned the divinity of the Spirit (and the Son). This more abstract problem grew out of the more concrete problem of the function of the Spirit in the Christian life. If the gift of the Spirit was only a sign of the end, the Spirit himself need not be fully divine. If the Spirit was another mediator, along with Christ, then his divinity was entailed. These problems paralleled yet another. If the Spirit was only an eschatological sign, then it was only meant for the eschatological community, the church.

Thus, some suggest that there is no concept in the New Testament of the Holy Spirit working outside of the fellowship of the church.[13] If this is true, then another effect of the increasing identification of the Spirit with the wisdom mediator and the Logos would be the increasing universalizing of the Spirit's activity, since the Logos was said to pervade everything.

Other scholars hold that the New Testament teaches both

a unique manifestation of the Spirit within the Christian community and a universal work of the Spirit beyond the church.[14] The tension of these two views of the Spirit's work (universal and confined to the Christian community) reflects the two motifs, wisdom and eschatology, with which we began.

If it is true that the Spirit's work is seen in the New Testament as taking place outside of the church, then the identification of the Spirit with the Logos and the inevitable universalizing of the Spirit is only a continuation of the New Testament doctrine. If, on the other hand, the New Testament confines the manifestations of the Holy Spirit to the Christian community, then the identification with the Logos might have been a necessary corrective to the overly sectarian emphasis of the New Testament writings. But it was a corrective bought at the price of the uniqueness of the Holy Spirit as a special gift to the followers of Christ. Thus, in the subsequent history of the church, any sense of the uniqueness of the working of the Holy Spirit and the importance of his special manifestation within the Christian community was often lost. The Holy Spirit became simply the term for the universal presence of God. Also, since most subsequent theology focused on the work of Christ, the nature of the Spirit's work became increasingly fuzzy. Discussion of the doctrine and work of the Third Person of the Trinity often paled before the theological attention lavished on the Second Person. All of these trends began in the early Patristic period and have continued to the present.

LIFE AND DOCTRINE: THOMAS AQUINAS

Son of a minor civil servant, Thomas Aquinas was born in Italy in 1225 and studied at the University of Naples. Around the age of twenty he entered the Dominican order and was sent to France to study under the most renowned theologian of the day, Albert the Great. Completing his course in theology in 1256 at the University of Paris, he joined the faculty there. In his thirties, his abilities were already recognized by the Dominicans and he was sent around to teach at several colleges in France and Italy. For these students he wrote the massive *Summa Theologica*, designed to combine the most rigorous philosophy and the best natural science of his day with the Christian faith. Aquinas died in 1274, on one of his many trips between France and Italy to take a new teaching post.

Aquinas inhabited a universe hierarchically arranged. Everything in this universe—the order of nature, the government of church and state, the structure of Christian theology—patterns itself neatly into a series of levels and stages. Feudal society had its nobles, knights, and peasants; the church its cardinals, bishops, priests, and laity. Christian thought had revealed theology, natural theology, and philosophy. Each rank is both superior to and built upon the one below it. Given this interdependence of all levels of the cosmic hierarchy, nothing moves from a lower rank to a higher one without the aid of a higher power. Only the people in the higher ranks of church or society could convey their authority or status to someone below; those below could not obtain it on their own. Only by supernatural revelation could natural theology be taken up into revealed theology.

In the same way, the possession of Christian faith was a supernatural state. The natural man could not attain it on his own but required the assistance of a supernatural agent. Even to prepare for this assisting grace man needed grace. To come to God man was dependent upon God. "A man cannot turn himself to God except through God turning him to himself," Aquinas wrote.[15] On this issue there is no difference between Thomas and the Reformers. Any view

of Reformation history that bases itself on a dichotomy
between the Reformers and Thomas on the issue of
justification must reexamine its premises. There is no
Pelagianism in Thomas. It is specifically condemned. The
only way to "merit" one's salvation is by God's grace, which
is no merit at all since "no creature can be a cause of
grace."[16]

For Thomas, God is absolutely sovereign and man is
redeemed by God's act alone. Any talk of man's meriting his
salvation or earning it himself is ruled out. The tendency in
the doctrine of justification by faith to make faith into a
"work" so that a man is justified by "believing" is rejected
by Thomas. "A man is justified by faith not in the sense that
he merits justification by believing but in the sense that he
believes while being justified," Thomas said.[17] For Thomas,
justification is *sola gratia.*

Thus, a man cannot move into the Christian life without
God moving him. What of living the Christian life? The
natural man, Thomas says, can do some good things but
they are of a very limited nature. He cannot even do "the
whole good which is natural to him." After the Fall, the
natural man needs the aid of God's grace just to do things
that should be natural to him.[18] Obviously the natural man
cannot do those supernaturally good works that comprise
the Christian life since, even on the purely natural level, to
perform these things that should be natural for him, he
needs the Holy Spirit. The Fall has meant that man cannot
"naturally" do what he was meant to do. Thus he, the
natural man, needs the Spirit of God just to bring him to
the place where he should be "naturally."

The work of the Spirit, then, is necessary to counteract
the Fall and make the natural man fully natural. It is also
necessary to bring a person to faith. Obviously, the work of
the Spirit is also needed in living the life of faith. Thomas

makes this point by distinguishing two types of virtues. There are the natural virtues, those that are in men by nature, but which need the Spirit to bring them to perfection. There are also the theological virtues, which, both in terms of their origin and perfection, come from the Holy Spirit. Thomas places the Christian life, which he describes as that "happiness surpassing man's nature and which man can obtain by the power of God alone,"[19] under the theological virtues. The Christian life, then, is a gift of the Spirit.

The theological virtues that form the basis of the Christian life are wholly the work of the Spirit of God since everything man receives from God must refer back to him. Thus God is both the efficient and the exemplary cause of the Christian life. He is the efficient cause because his Spirit moves men to do the works of the Christian life. He is the exemplary cause because the Christian life must be a life reflecting the nature of God. The Christian life is not just a matter of doing good works, for the natural man can do them, too (although not without the aid of grace). The Christian life must exemplify and point to God "that the Father may be glorified in the Son."

The "gifts of the Holy Spirit," Thomas says, are given to perfect the theological virtues. Each Christian receives the theological virtues through the Holy Spirit. Then he receives these gifts of the Spirit "to remedy certain defects."[20] The theological virtues are the "roots" of the gifts of the Spirit. The purpose of these gifts is to perfect man, so that he is able to follow the leading of the Spirit. By tying the gifts of the Spirit so tightly to the theological virtues, Thomas implies that, although the Spirit is a universal agent of God, the specific gifts of the Spirit are a function of the Christian life alone.

The theological virtues, then, form the context of the gifts of the Spirit. Charity, which encompasses all the gifts of the Spirit, is the greatest of the theological virtues. No one can possess the gifts of the Spirit without love. Unlike some exegetes, Thomas does not confuse what Paul calls the gifts of the Spirit (1 Cor. 12) with the fruits of the Spirit (Gal. 5:22), although he refers to the latter as "virtues." Like Paul, Thomas asserts that the purpose of the gifts of the Spirit is to manifest the fruits of the Spirit. Thus, he says, the gifts of the Spirit are perfected in love.

Thus, the goal of the work of the Spirit is love. The gifts of the Spirit are not only given instrumentally (as a means to an end) but first of all simply as an expression of the divine love for man. The Holy Spirit, as the manifestation of the divine love, gives the love of God to men so that men will both be loved by God and enabled to love God. Therefore, Thomas writes, "the love with which God loves us pertains to the Holy Ghost: also the love with which we love God, since it is he who makes us lovers of God."[21] The Spirit, which is the divine love, is the source of all the virtues and gifts that make up the Christian life because, for Thomas, the Christian life is summed up in love.

The Holy Spirit also plays a part in what Thomas calls the final goal of the Christian life: The contemplation of God. Man's contemplation of God must grow out of the love of God, Thomas says. Here Thomas is using the phrase "love of God" in a twofold sense: It refers both to God's love of mankind and man's return of that love to God. Since the Holy Spirit is another name for divine love, the Spirit is obviously the primary agent in contemplation. The Holy Spirit provides that experience of the love of God that turns men to God and moves them to contemplation. The Spirit also infuses the divine love into men, which fills them with the love that they can return to God in contemplation.

Thomas's discussion of the work of the Spirit presupposes that the Spirit is the divine love, for the work of the Spirit is communicating the love of God to men. Thomas's view of the work of the Spirit follows naturally from his conception of the Trinity. Thomas, like Augustine, models the Trinity on the human mind. The mind, he says, has three parts: (1) the mind itself, (2) the reasoning faculty, and (3) the will that puts the conclusions of reason into action. The reason and the will are not separate from the mind as a whole, rather they are manifestations (Thomas calls them "processions") of the mind. Reason is the mind manifesting itself in thought; will is the mind manifesting itself in action.

As in the human mind, so in God—there is one procession of intellect and one procession of will. The procession of the intellect is the divine Word, which is God's "intelligent operation."[22] The procession of the will is love, the principle of divine operation, which is the Holy Spirit. A procession in God must not be defined in terms of something outside of God, since Thomas holds Aristotle's definition of the self-contained God. The procession of the will in God can only be love because love is the only act of the will that need not relate to anything beyond itself. The Holy Spirit is the love by which God loves himself for only thus can the object and the source of the will be the same.

Every rational creature has a will. This will exists according to the nature of that creature. For Thomas, then, the will is the expression of the nature of the self in action. God has a will, too. Scripture says that God is love. Therefore his will must be love. The volitional element in the Godhead is the Holy Spirit, whose nature is the divine nature, which is love. Reason and revelation overlap. Reason dictates that the will of God must be love, for only then could it have its source for its object. Scripture says that the divine nature is love, which entails that his will must also be love, since the divine will has the same nature as God himself. Reason and revelation agree that the Holy Spirit must be the love of God.

The Trinity is united because the Three Persons are expressions of the same common divinity, just as the mind, the reason, and the will are expressions of the common mind. How, then, are the Three Persons distinguished? Thomas says they are distinguished by their relations to each other. The only interrelation there can be in God, Thomas says, is that of origin. The Father is the origin of the Son and the Spirit just as the mind is the ground of the reason and the will. But if this is not to be simply binitarianism, one of these two must be the origin of the other. Scripture does not support the view that the Spirit is the origin of the Son, Thomas says; but it does support the view that the Son is the origin of the Spirit. Thus the Son and the Spirit are distinguished by relation, the Son is the origin of the Spirit.

Thomas emphasizes the procession of the Spirit from the Son not as a polemic against the Eastern church, which rejects this position and says that the Spirit proceeds only from the Father. Rather, his whole doctrine of the Trinity depends on it. If the Spirit does not proceed from the Son, there is no way of distinguishing them since relations of origin are the only ones allowable in the Godhead. The Holy Spirit, then, proceeds from the Father through the Son. The Son receives from the Father the power to generate the Spirit. Both the Spirit and the Son are from the Father but the Spirit is from the Father through the Son. Such a close connection of the Spirit to the Son might entail that the work of the Spirit takes place under the work of the

Son. This would push Thomas in the direction of limiting the work of the Spirit to the Christian community. On the other hand, by defining the Spirit as the manifestation of the Godhead in action the Spirit's work is universalized, since the action of God embraces the whole creation. That part of Thomas's Trinitarian doctrine that binds the Spirit to the Son points in the direction of viewing the Spirit as a special endowment of Christians; that part of his doctrine that defines the Spirit as the divine volition universalizes the Spirit's scope.

The practical importance of Thomas's doctrine of the Trinity for understanding the work of the Spirit becomes clear when Thomas defines the processions within the Godhead as "divine missions." A mission is a functional term as well as a philosophical one. It refers both to the relation of God to the world and the relations within the Godhead. The mission of a Person of the Trinity is defined by his nature. He is given his existence out of the divine source by his mission. There is no distinction between economic and ontological views of the Trinity.[23] The nature of the Holy Spirit is also the function of the Holy Spirit. The nature is love; his work is love.

Our discussion of the work of the Spirit led inevitably to the doctrine of the Trinity. The Thomistic doctrine of the Trinity led inevitably back to the work of the Spirit. The nature of the Spirit's work is love, which reflects his nature within the Trinity. The function of the Spirit's work is to move the world in accordance with the divine love, which reflects his mission within the Trinity. Thus Thomas says that those supernatural endowments, which Paul calls the gifts of the Spirit, are given the believer both as an expression of God's love for him and to enable him to, in turn, love God as well. When the gifts of the Spirit are given, a person is aimed in the direction of the divine will. Moved by the Spirit, formed in love, the person is pointed toward God, who is love. Since the Spirit is an expression of the nature, character, and activity of God, to partake in the Spirit is to partake in the very nature of God, to be formed after the divine character, and to be directed in the direction of the divine will.

For Thomas, the agent through which God (not in the sense of the Father but in the sense of the entire Godhead) works is the Spirit. The Spirit, for Thomas, is the procession of God according to will. Since the will is the agent of activity for the mind, the Spirit is the form in which the Godhead becomes active. The work of the Father in creation was accomplished through the Spirit who "brooded upon the waters." The Son's direct work was redemption; but the Son now sits at the right hand of God and rules. He rules through the Spirit, for the Spirit proceeds from both the Father and the Son. The work of the Spirit is a universal work. It is the name given to the Godhead in action. But it is also a particular work, done with a particular form (love) and for a particular end (union with God). Linked with the particular revelation in Jesus the Son, the work of the Spirit manifests itself in particular virtues and gifts. In his doctrine of the Trinity, Thomas is struggling with the problem we have seen inherent in the doctrine of the Spirit from the time of the early church—how to balance the universal and particular working of the Spirit.

THE DELICATE DIALECTIC: JOHN CALVIN

Born in France in 1509, John Calvin was the son of a well-to-do lawyer, who originally intended his son to be a priest but later sent him to study law. Completing these studies, Calvin went to Paris to learn arts and philosophy. There is no evidence that he took up theology directly, and many theologians have been disciples of this man who never specifically studied theology. While engaged in these general studies, Calvin underwent a dramatic and unexpected conversion, which turned him toward reform of the Catholic church in Europe. When a close friend, Nicholas Cop, became rector of the University of Paris and spoke out forcefully for reform, he was driven from Paris, and Calvin was exiled along with him. In hiding, Calvin wrote his major systematic work, *Institutes of the Christian Religion*, in an attempt to explain the Reformation to the King of France and end the persecution of Protestants there.

Fleeing from place to place, Calvin came to Geneva; recently converted to reform under William Farel, Geneva was in chaos. Farel insisted Calvin stay and Calvin immediately set to work reorganizing the church and enforcing strict morals on the citizens. His stern measures provoked so much opposition that two years later he was driven from Geneva into exile again. With his departure, disorder returned and three years later he was recalled. Returning, he clamped down harder than before, until he made Geneva a model for the Reformation throughout Europe. For over twenty years Calvin continued as pastor to the city—preaching, teaching, visiting the sick, advising the city council—until May 1564, when he died and was buried, at his own request, in an unmarked grave in Geneva.

Apart from the perception of man's total dependence upon God, Calvin's theology is meaningless. For Calvin, as for Thomas, no man can bring himself to God. Man's reason is corrupted by sin, Calvin says, and thus only falls into idolatry and confusion when it seeks God. Although there is a potential revelation of God in his creation, man's vision is so darkened that he cannot see it. Therefore God must provide man with another revelation, which sets forth the nature of God "truly and vividly." Thus God gives man the Scripture as a gift of grace. The Bible is itself grace. It is a divine gift to man to enable him to do that which he cannot do for himself. For Calvin the Scriptures not only tell of grace but are themselves the graceful answer to man's Fall.

However, the book of Scripture is not enough by itself. Man's mind and will still suffer the effects of the Fall. Because of the bondage of his will to sin, man cannot turn himself toward God's revelation. And, because his mind has also been affected by the Fall, he is unable to comprehend God's truth even if this truth is set before him. Despite man's intentions, the weakness of his will and the darkness of his mind paralyze him. Overcoming these defects is part of the work of the Spirit. According to Calvin, the Holy Spirit redirects the will toward God's revelation and illuminates the mind to understand God's truth.

But this is still not enough. The Scriptures can be given as a guide to fallen man. The Spirit can be given to strengthen his will and lighten his mind to turn to the Bible. The question still remains, why should he? There is no clear reason why man should turn to the Scriptures. The Bible may be revelatory, but the grounds of that revelation and the reason why it should be accepted are not immediately apparent just from the text of the book. What is its authority? Again, there is a need for the work of the Spirit. The Spirit must clarify the authority of the Scripture.

Calvin is clear that the Scripture is the work of the Spirit. But simply being a work of the Spirit does not validate the Scripture. Authority, for Calvin, does not lie in something being simply a work of the Spirit. For Calvin, authority lies in something being confirmed as authoritative in the heart of the individual.[24] For Calvin man is divided into the mind, the will, and the heart (the locus of the emotions). The mind cannot give certainty, Calvin says, because its knowledge always comes through the senses and is therefore subject to doubt. The will can give no certainty either for it is dependent upon the mind. But the heart is the seat of certainty and assurance for Calvin. For the mind to grasp the ideas in Scripture is not enough, this does not insure their certainty or authority. For the will to hold fast to the Scripture is not enough, either, for this entails no certainty of their truth. But, for Calvin, the testimony of the heart points to authority and leads to certainty.

The work of the Spirit in giving man the Scripture as a guide to his corrupted reason and weakened will is a threefold work, which corresponds to the threefold nature of man as Calvin saw it. Regarding reason, the Spirit illuminates it to ascertain the truth in the Scriptures. "Without the illumination of the Holy Spirit, the Word can do nothing."[25] Regarding the will, the Spirit empowers the will to be able to turn toward the divine revelation. Regarding the heart, the Spirit confirms within the heart the authority of Scripture. "Scripture is self-authenticating. . . . The certainty it deserves with us, it attains by testimony of the Spirit."[26]

Calvin here has two polemical objectives. He reasons that, because the Spirit wrote the Scriptures, they are authenticated when the same Spirit testifies to them within the heart. This means that the Scripture is independent of any human or institutional support. Calvin can use the Scripture as a contravailing authority against the Roman church since Scripture's authority is not dependent upon the church. But since the Spirit wrote the Scripture, he is subject to the Scripture. Scripture provides the norm for judging the works of the Spirit. It is not a tyrannical norm; it is the Spirit's own norm. Since the Spirit inspired the Scriptures and since he cannot be inconsistent with himself, they are the norm he himself created. Therefore the Scripture can be used to keep those sectarian groups, who claimed the Spirit led them beyond the teachings of the New Testament, in line. With his view of the Scripture's authority, Calvin is able to fend off attacks from the Roman church on one side and the Anabaptist sects on the other.

The work of the Spirit in inspiring and authenticating the Scriptures and turning men to them is not an end in itself. It is a means to the chief end of the work of the Spirit, the creation of faith. The Scripture is given man to bring him to faith. According to Calvin, faith is made up of knowledge (based on the Scripture) and union with Christ. In the creation of faith, the stages of the Spirit's work correspond to Calvin's understanding of man.

Regarding the element of knowledge, the Spirit illuminates the mind and secures the truth in the heart. The mind, sunk in sin, cannot understand the principles upon which faith depends. It must, therefore, be illuminated by the Spirit. In bringing men to faith, the Spirit's work of illumination is not confined to the Scripture. It is needed whenever men try to know God: In the teachings of the church, the preaching of the Word, as well as the reading of Scripture. In commenting on the passage, "no one can say Jesus is Lord except by the Holy Spirit," Calvin remarks that this "illumination" is not "a common endowment of nature" but is a supernatural gift of the Spirit, which is necessary even for this elementary confession of faith.[27] Men must understand, Calvin says, "that the way to the Kingdom of God is open only to him whose mind has been renewed by the illumination of the Holy Spirit."[28] Even in Christ's preaching, and by implication in man's also, "nothing is accomplished" unless the Spirit, "our inner teacher," is present.[29] Nor can man make the right moral decisions unless illuminated by the Spirit.

There is more to faith, for Calvin, than simply understanding of and commitment to the principles of truth. This relates to the mind but there are also those elements of faith that relate to the heart. They involve the certainty of the truth as well as the understanding of it.[30]

> It now remains to pour into the heart itself what the mind has absorbed. For the Word of God is not received by faith if it flits about in the top of the brain but when it takes root in the depth of the heart. . . . if it is true that the mind's real understanding is illumination by the Spirit of God, then in such confirmation of the heart his power is much more clearly manifested. . . . It is harder for the heart to be furnished with assurance than for the mind to be endowed with thought.[31]

This second work of the Spirit in the creation of faith (giving assurance in the heart) is more important for Calvin than the first (giving the mind understanding). He concludes that "the knowledge of faith consists in certainty rather than in comprehension."[32] The Spirit completes the work begun in its illumination of the mind by a second and more important work: Giving the heart certainty about the truth of its faith. "The commencement of faith is knowledge; the completion of it is a firm and fixed persuasion which admits no opposing doubts. Both are works of the Spirits."[33]

Faith is more than knowledge, however certain. It is also union with Christ. Knowledge is only the first step in man's union with God. In knowledge alone, "Christ, so to speak, lies idle because we coldly contemplate him as outside ourselves—indeed far from us."[34] Apart from a spiritual as well as an intellectual union with Christ, there can be no appropriation of freedom and redemption. This final stage of faith (union with Christ) is also wholly a work of the Spirit. "He unites himself to us by the Spirit alone."[35] Thus the Holy Spirit functions as a kind of mediator between Christ and man, just as Christ functions as a mediator between God and man. "The Holy Spirit is the bond," Calvin writes, "by which Christ effectually unites us to himself."[36]

Since the Spirit mediates between Christ and the believer, the Spirit, too, may be called a mediator, perhaps "comediatrix." The use of this term from Mariology may point out why Calvin needed the Spirit to serve in this way as another mediator. It has been suggested that one of the reasons Mariology arose in the late medieval period was because the figure of Jesus became more and more distant, both theologically and devotionally, from the rest of mankind.[37] Heavy emphasis on Jesus as a Divine Being, fully revealing the glory of God and painfully bearing the sins of the entire world, made him seem remote from the rest of mankind. This remoteness of Christ created a need for a mediator between him and the rest of humanity, a need that was filled by a very human rendering of the Virgin Mary.

The late medieval church applied the category of Sophia to Mary. Before, we saw how the categories of wisdom played an important part in the development of the doctrine of the Spirit as mediator. Therefore Mary took on, in some late medieval Mariology, the functions traditionally assigned to the Spirit.[38] This is not a new Trinitarianism but simply the assumption on Mary's part of some of the images formerly applied to the Third Person of the Trinity. It is tempting to suggest that the same forces that drove late medieval thought toward Mariology also formed Calvin's pneumatology (since he rejected any Mariology). This would be oversimplified, but it would point out that the Spirit functions as a mediator for Calvin in much the same way that Mary did for medieval Catholicism.

Theologically, Calvin's Christ is somewhat remote from mankind. This remoteness comes from Calvin's almost total limitation of Christ's work to the atonement. This work of the atonement is tied to the once and for all, and thoroughly past, event of the Cross. The primary work of Christ is seen as occurring in the past, out of direct reach of men in the present. In the present, Christ reigns in heaven. But as a polemic against the Lutherans, whose sacramental doctrine presupposed that Christ was directly and universally present in the world, Calvin emphasized that Christ was directly present only in heaven. Calvin's heavy emphasis on the Cross and his limitation of Christ's immediate presence to the Heavenly Kingdom created the need for a mediator between Christ and mankind.

Philosophically, Calvin's need for a mediator between Christ and the rest of mankind came out of the breakdown of scholastic philosophy under the attack of the so-called "nominalists" in the late medieval period. High medieval theologians, like Thomas Aquinas, held that there was a universal human nature in which all men participate and share in common. Thus Christ, simply by taking on himself the nature of man, united himself, at least in potential, to all men through this bond of a common, human "nature." The nominalist attack, from which their name comes, consisted in demonstrating that there were no such universal natures. Universals (like "human nature") were simply "names" for groups of individual things. Christ became a particular, individual man. That in no way united him to other men, who were also only particular individuals and not participants in a common nature. Calvin had to find another way to unite Christ to mankind without reference to the philosophically bankrupt concept of a universal human nature.

The Spirit mediates Christ to man and unites him with the believer. The final goal of the work of the Spirit is man's union with Christ, which Calvin calls faith. In faith "Christ is outside us but dwells within us. Not only does he cleave to us by an invisible bond of fellowship but by a wonderful communion day by day he grows more and more into one body with us, until he becomes completely one with us."[39] It is almost as if Calvin had taken the medieval theology of the Sacraments and applied it to the work of the Spirit. In his *Commentary on John*, chapter 14, Calvin says that Christ is known through faith, which is "the sacred and mysterious union between us and him; but the only way of knowing this is when he diffuses his life into us by the secret efficacy of the Spirit." To further the suggestion that Calvin uses traditional Sacramental images to explain his doctrine of the Spirit, it should be noted that in the same *Commentary on John*, in reference to verse 6:53, Calvin says that the union that Jesus describes here "does not relate to the Lord's Supper but to that perpetual communion which we obtain apart from the use of the Lord's Supper." The Sacrament is thus made a symbol of that "perpetual communion" that the believer always enjoys with Christ through the Spirit. Union with Christ in this more universalistic and spiritual sense is represented in the particular act of breaking bread.[40] The scriptural images for the breaking of bread can therefore be applied to that union through the Spirit, of which the Sacrament is a symbol.

Calvin's treatment of the Spirit is practical throughout. Calvin quickly passes over the metaphysical arguments that occupied such a large place in Thomas's *Summa Theologica*. Calvin only briefly discusses the metaphysics of the doctrine of the Trinity. He says, in much the same way as Thomas, that the Scripture witnesses to the deity of the Spirit and implies that the "Spirit is an entity subsisting in God." The Spirit, Calvin writes, "resides hypostatically in God." These terms are not elaborated. Calvin's interests are elsewhere, but he does include the traditional formula in the *Institutes*.

For Calvin, as for Thomas, the Spirit appears as the Godhead in action. The Spirit was an agent in Creation for "the universe was no less the work of the Holy Spirit than of the Son."[41] Calvin discusses Providence under the topic of Creation. Thus he ascribes to the Spirit an active part in both the Creation and preservation of the world. "The beauty of the universe owes its strength and preservation to the power of the Spirit" Calvin says in his exegesis of Gen. 1:2.[42] Calvin also writes:

> It is the Spirit who, everywhere diffused, sustains all things, causes them to grow, and quickens them in heaven and in earth. Because he is circumscribed by no limits, he is excepted from the category of creatures; but in transfusing into all things his energy, and breathing into them essence, life, and movement, he is indeed plainly divine.[43]

Calvin identifies the Holy Spirit with the immanence of God and therefore implies that the Spirit's work is universal. Not only immanent in nature, Calvin also suggests that the Spirit is given to all men. His exegesis of 1 cor. 12:6 suggests that the Spirit is at work in everyone and is the cause of whatever good is done, by Christians and non-Christians. All science and learning, he says, as well as theology and morality come from the Holy Spirit.

— For Calvin, then, the Spirit's work is both universal and particular. The Spirit is the immanent power of God at work in all creation. But the most important work of the Spirit, for Calvin, is bringing men into union with Christ. It is this particular work of the Spirit that makes sense of the larger work. Without the particular illumination of the Spirit, man cannot perceive the universal presence. Without the particular knowledge, which comes through Jesus Christ, man cannot understand the universal action of God.

The Spirit's work is both universal and particular; it is also, therefore, both objective and subjective. The Spirit works subjectively, within man's heart and mind. But Calvin does not identify the work of the Spirit with man's thoughts and feelings. Rather the Spirit is grounded in the Scripture, the historical Jesus, who is the reigning Lord of the spiritual community, and the action of God in nature. The Spirit is not to provide men rich internal experiences but to point them beyond their subjectivity to the Word, the Lord, the church, and the action of God in Creation and history.

THE LIBERAL SPIRIT: F. E. D. SCHLEIERMACHER

Born into a close-knit community of German Brethren in 1768, Friedrich Schleiermacher was raised in this intensely pious atmosphere until, rebelling against the intellectual confinements of the Moravian Brethren, he went off to the University of Halle. Although within the Pietist tradition,

Halle was open to the skepticism and rationalism of the Enlightenment and there Schleiermacher gave himself to philosophy. In 1796 he moved to Berlin and became intimate in a literary circle busily assimilating the Romantic movement with its emphasis on emotion and aesthetics. The Romantic concern with feeling recalled Schleiermacher's early piety and he sought to combine them in a book entitled *On Religion* (1799), which joined Christian theology with the Romantic ideal of religion as a type of sensibility—a sense and feeling for the universal. Leaving Berlin for a country pastorate, he soon returned to Halle as professor of theology and preacher to the university. Two years later, as he finally became settled there, Napoleon invaded Germany and dissolved the university. The hope of continuing his career destroyed, Schleiermacher returned to Berlin and was soon engaged in founding the University of Berlin, where he lectured alongside the greatest philosopher of the time, Hegel. Beside lecturing on ethics, theology, philosophy, church history, New Testament, and pastoral care, Schleiermacher was deeply involved in the Prussian Academy, making a considerable contribution to the study of Greek philosophy. A vigorous proponent of German nationalism, he was a frequent preacher against French encroachments on Germany; he also drew up a plan for uniting Lutherans and Calvinists in Germany. Twelve years before his death in 1834, Schleiermacher published *The Christian Faith*, a systematic attempt to reconstruct the doctrines of Christianity to take account of the skeptical philosophies of the Enlightenment, the historical criticism of scripture, and the Romantic sensibility, which has inspired generations of "liberal" theologians in Germany and America.

For Schleiermacher, as for Calvin, the experience of

redemption is a lens that brings the different facets of Christian thought into focus. Neither Schleiermacher nor Calvin begin their works with the doctrine of redemption (both begin with man's knowledge of God). Both place the consideration of redemption at the center of their dogmatics, so that it can throw its light in all directions. Whatever diverse "natural" knowledge of God man may possess, the experience of redemption illuminates it, gathers it together, and projects it onward as the narrow beam of the Christian life. Calvin says that it is only through the Scriptures and the Spirit that man can truly know God. Schleiermacher says that only Christ can reform man's natural consciousness of God into the shape of truth.

For Schleiermacher, man begins the pilgrimage toward faith with some awareness of the divine. Religion arises in that sphere of existence where the self becomes present to itself. In the experience of self-awareness, man realizes that he did not create himself, but rather that his own existence and existence in general are gifts to him. In relation to his point of origin, man feels absolutely dependent on something outside of himself as the source of that life, which he knows he could not have given to himself. For Schleiermacher, the term "God" designates this sense. God is the name given to the object of man's basal consciousness of absolute dependence on something beyond himself as the source of that which he did not create for himself—his own existence.

This consciousness of God is not fully developed in human life. A fully developed God-consciousness would mean that at every moment man would be conscious of God; or, as Schleiermacher puts it, man's consciousness of God and his consciousness of the world would coincide. At every moment he would be conscious of God and the world together. Thus God-consciousness would fill man's entire being. The term for the impairment of the full consciousness of God, Schleiermacher says, is "sin." The natural man tends to focus only on the world, on the transitory, and thus blocks the full realization of the consciousness of God. For Schleiermacher, as for Calvin, the essence of sin is idolatry, attending to the finite in the place of the divine. For both Calvin and Schleiermacher the consciousness of sin has so come to dominate the mind of the natural man that he is incapable of seeing either the world or God correctly. Because of sin the world obscures God rather than revealing him; God is perceived as an enemy or an unknown rather than as a friend.

Redemption is always defined in Christian dogmatics as the antithesis of sin. For Schleiermacher, redemption is accomplished by one in whom the consciousness of God is not obscured at all but rather permeates his entire being. He is sinless and needs no redemption. By the power of his God-consciousness the redeemer turns men to himself. What does it mean that he attracts them other than that their consciousness of God is brought into line with his own. Thereby they, too, enter the state of redemption.

The presence of God himself makes Christ the redeemer; not his own personality or teachings but "the being of God within him." This is what he passes on to others. Jesus is the pattern on which the redeemed are reformed. This transformation of character is not an act of their own will; it is accomplished by the power of God at work both within them and within Christ. To say that Jesus is a pattern is not to reduce him to an ideal, which men may choose to follow or not. What is manifest in this image is the power of God himself, which Jesus conveys to all men.

Jesus' relation to his followers is not that of teacher to

pupil but of creator to creature. By the power of his consciousness of God he alters their state of consciousness to such an extent that they become a "new creation." They in turn then possess the power of so influencing others, who in turn can so influence many more. For Schleiermacher, the doctrine of the coming of the Spirit and the church is not something tacked onto the end of his dogmatics as it often appears to be in those Protestant theologians, where the Cross becomes so central that everything appears dogmatically downhill from there. Rather the Spirit and the church flow necessarily from the wellspring of salvation. Christ's influence leads inevitably to a new consciousness, which must express itself in a new community that carries on his work.

What Christ leaves behind, then, is a new community. The picture in Schleiermacher's dogmatics corresponds almost exactly with the account in the Book of Acts. The disciples are bound together by a new experience of the presence and power of God, a presence and power they both perceived in Jesus and received through him. New members are brought into the community and redemption is extended through this same presence in this community. The redeemed God-consciousness now resides in the whole community rather than in one man, Jesus. The power of Jesus' consciousness of God was so great that it drew out the potential God-consciousness in those associated with him and brought it into harmony with his own. Since these followers now possess the "mind of Christ" they can do the same for others who are thus drawn into association with them. These new followers can, in turn, so influence others. Thus the church is formed and the work of Christ extended.

The church is the extension of the Incarnation. On the basis of the redeeming power, which Christ once exercised directly and now exercises indirectly through the Spirit-filled community, the work of redemption is carried out. Again, the picture is that of Luke, for whom Christ's personal influence has ceased and the work of the Spirit has taken over. For Luke, this is due to the Ascension, whereas for Schleiermacher Christ's death is the end of his direct work. After his death, his work is carried out by the new consciousness in his disciples.

By the terms of his own dogmatics, Schleiermacher is forced to confront the same questions on the relation of the Spirit to the church that were raised earlier in terms of the exegesis of the New Testament. The Holy Spirit is identified with that potency of God-consciousness found first in Christ and then in the church. Schleiermacher is driven to resolve exegetical problems on dogmatic grounds. He must identify the Spirit with the Son and also limit the Spirit to the church. Schleiermacher therefore gives a clear and strong dogmatic expression of the Lukan tradition, which sees the Spirit as a special gift to the church, and the Pauline emphasis on the close connection of the Spirit to the building up of the community.

For Schleiermacher, the Holy Spirit is the theological name given to the communal spirit of fellowship found in the church. Every human organization has its "common spirit" (*Gemeingeist*). For Schleiermacher, this is especially true of the body politic. For Schleiermacher, the state (that is, the culture as well as the government) is a "moral personality." The culture and government of a commonwealth are expressions of the moral personality or the "spirit" of that society. In the same way the structure and ethos of the church are expressions of its corporate personality, which is the Holy Spirit. The Spirit, then, is both the cause of the community, since it is the communication of the Spirit from Jesus, which creates the church, and an expression of its common life.

This obviously entails that the Holy Spirit *per se* belongs only to the church. Schleiermacher explicitly argues that the New Testament ascribes the Spirit only to believers. The Holy Spirit of Christian experience is not, for Schleiermacher, the same Spirit whom the Old Testament describes as present at creation or as speaking through the prophets. Schleiermacher is always suspicious of too close a connection of Christianity with Judaism, for fear that such a connection would undermine the uniqueness of Christianity. Since each culture is a corporate personality, it has its own Spirit; but one ought not be "compelled to identify the common Spirit of the Jewish theocracy with that of the Christian church."[44]

Having preserved the uniqueness of Christianity by sundering it from the Old Testament, Schleiermacher goes on to suggest that since the Holy Spirit is the fellowship of the church, it cannot strictly be said to have been present at the time of the Incarnation. Here Schleiermacher is on shakier ground dogmatically, since he previously said that the Holy Spirit is what Jesus communicated to his disciples. Therefore, it must be something present with him. But Schleiermacher's intent is clear: To identify the Spirit so closely with the common life of the church that everything that takes place in the church, all the gifts of the Spirit, can be traced through the Spirit directly to Christ as the fountainhead of the Christian life. In the neoorthodox theology of the turn of this century, which followed Karl Barth and Emil Brunner, it was fashionable to criticize Schleiermacher for undermining the centrality of Christ and the uniqueness of Christianity. However, in Schleiermacher's discussion of the nature of the church and the work of the Spirit, his intention is to emphasize the uniqueness of the Christian life and to derive it solely from Christ.

This identification of the Spirit with the church means that Schleiermacher is able to express more forcefully than Calvin the Pauline theme of the work of the Spirit in the building up of the community. Calvin so closely allied the work of the Spirit with the work of Christ on the Cross that bringing men to the experience of salvation became the primary work of the Third Person of the Trinity. Schleiermacher, too, emphasizes this. But in Schleiermacher the individualistic nature of the experience of redemption is balanced by a sense of the corporate nature of the Christian life, which is often missing in Protestant theology, both liberal and evangelical. Since the Holy Spirit is the corporate Spirit of the community, it is essential to the work of the Spirit that men be formed into the Body of Christ. The Spirit's work is not complete with the application of redemption to the individual; it is not complete until men are formed into community.

Protestant theology is here more apt to follow St. Thomas than St. Paul. Aquinas, as we saw, said that the gifts of the Spirit belong to each individual to enable him to perfect the Christian theological virtues in his own life. St. Paul implies that the gifts of the Spirit belong to the body and to each individual only to the extent that he participates in the Christian community. Thomas and Calvin obviously do not neglect the importance of the church. But for them the gifts of the Spirit are predicated primarily of the individual and the church is seen as drawing its spiritual power from that of the Spirit-filled people who make it up. However, for Paul, the Spirit is predicated primarily of the Body of Christ and each individual derives his spiritual power from participating in the Body. Here Schleiermacher, with his emphasis on the Spirit's work in creating community, may be a more faithful expositor of St. Paul than certain, more traditional, dogmatics.

Another exegetical problem that the early church passed on to its descendents is the relation of the Spirit to Christ. The initial ambiguity of the primitive church on this matter was clarified in the ensuing debates, which led to the formation of the doctrine of the Trinity. Schleiermacher makes no theological use of the doctrine of the Trinity. This radical theological rejection ironically frees him to return to at least some of the distinctive themes in the pneumatology of the early church. One of these is the close identification of the Spirit with Christ, which we noted in some patristic writings, and which the doctrine of the Trinity tends to mitigate by making them separate "Persons." Since the potency of Christ's God-consciousness is what is transferred from Christ to the community under the title of the Holy Spirit, to be "in Christ" and to have the Spirit are, for Schleiermacher, two terms for the same reality.[45] This is the same position found in St. Paul. For Schleiermacher the community arises only from Christ, and therefore its common life (i.e., the Holy Spirit) is identical with his.

This, then, is Schleiermacher's ground for asserting the Divinity of the Spirit. In Christ, everything proceeds from the being of God (his God-consciousness) within him. This obviously includes the life of the church, the redeemed life, which is derived most intimately from his own life. Thus the Spirit, the communication of that interior consciousness of Christ, which Schleiermacher has called divine, is also divine. This way of affirming the divinity of the Spirit by basing it so strictly on the divinity of Christ and the identification of Christ with the Spirit, might lead to the paradoxical (from the standpoint of what Schleiermacher calls "Protestant dogmatics") conclusion that the church is divine. This, too, might not be too far from the mind of St. Paul, who speaks of the church (as he does the eucharistic offering) as the Body of Christ. For both Paul and Schleiermacher the life of the community is intimately bound up with the divine life of Christ and his Spirit.

Thus, for Schleiermacher, there is no salvation outside of the church. To be redeemed is synonymous with becoming a member of the community. Following Calvin, Schleiermacher says that redemption means entering into fellowship with Christ through the work of the Spirit. What Schleiermacher means by entering into fellowship with Christ is, however, entering the community. Christ's direct influence ceased with his death. Now his influence continues through the redeemed community, which possesses the same redeeming potency of God-consciousness that was in him. The only way one can now come in contact with this redeeming power is through the community. Thus, as Schleiermacher writes, "being drawn into the fellowship of believers, having a share in the Holy Spirit, and being drawn into fellowship with Christ—must simply mean one and the same thing."[46] Although sanctification is progressive, there are no stages in the Christian life. Believing in Christ, receiving the Holy Spirit, and joining the community are different names for the same event.

Here again Schleiermacher may be closer than many more orthodox theologians to the New Testament teaching that there is no real experience of life in Christ apart from the immediate and experiential reception of the Holy Spirit and entrance into the church.[47] The Scripture does not say, as Schleiermacher does, that receiving the Spirit is simply another name for believing in Christ. In Luke and Paul, belief in Christ is an event that entails immediately the experiential reception of the Holy Spirit. Schleiermacher simultaneously affirms and undermines the New Testament emphasis on the Spirit. He affirms it by emphasizing that there is no full Christian life apart from a conscious life in the Spirit. He undermines it by making it easy to equate the supranatural gifts of the Spirit with the human confession of faith in Jesus, although that was not his intent, for he makes it clear that reception of the Spirit and therefore the confession of faith is not a human act but an experience of a power beyond the natural man.

This raises another consideration of Schleiermacher's doctrine of the Spirit. The Spirit is not something external to man, something that influences him from outside of himself. The work of the Spirit "is determined from within [*innen*] and only this . . . is the sphere of the Holy Spirit."[48] Schleiermacher rejects those passages of Scripture that seem to picture the Spirit as an external influence, as one that is over against man and that relates to him as another personal existence.[49] He says these passages derive their imagery too closely from the language of the Old Testament prophets. Christian doctrine, he says, stresses gifts of the Spirit, which reside wholly within men. The Holy Spirit is divine in that he is derived from Christ. But he is a wholly immanent feature of human life. To say that the Holy Spirit is not entirely "bound up" with human nature, Schleiermacher warns, would be to "sunder the unity of [man's] being . . . [and to] produce so entire a dualism within human life that it could never be maintained."[50]

Schleiermacher's argument has gotten the best of him. He wants to maintain that the Holy Spirit is not an external force that overpowers man's natural faculties and possesses them as demons are pictured as doing in the synoptic gospels. To maintain that the Holy Spirit is not inimical to human nature he goes to the opposite extreme of suggesting that the Spirit is not beyond man at all. Thus Schleiermacher confuses the gifts of the Spirit with the Spirit himself. The gifts of the Spirit are pictured by Paul as residing within men and being made a part of their personalities. That does not mean that the Spirit himself is so pictured. The Spirit, for Paul, remains a free, sovereign, divine person. Schleiermacher's overpowering but understandable drive to refute any dualism (particularly between the natural and the supernatural) causes him only to emphasize the Spirit's immanence and thereby distort the teaching he is trying to defend. He defends the Lukan and Pauline theme, which makes experiencing the Spirit a definitive part of the Christian life. But he distorts this experience by so emphasizing the human, psychological qualities of the Spirit's work that it is hard to understand in what sense the Spirit is a divine and not only a human reality.

For Schleiermacher, then, the Holy Spirit is a human potential that is the same in all men. It is the potential for sharing in the common life of the church. It is the potential for full God-consciousness. This potential is awakened and made actual by contact with the community in which this common life and God-consciousness is already actualized. Each may have different gifts; that is, each may actualize this potential in a way fitting to his own personality; but all partake in the same Spirit. That is, this potential is the same in all men, even apart from redemption.[51] Although Schleiermacher confines the work of the Spirit *per se* only to the church, he here introduces a universality of the potential for the Holy Spirit.

This, too, is not out of keeping with the Lukan tradition, for in Acts Peter says that the promise of the Spirit is to all men. But, because Schleiermacher has so emphasized the human aspect of the Spirit's work, it is hard to understand the relation of this potential to the Spirit himself. Schleiermacher seems to imply that this is not a potential to receive the Spirit but is the Spirit himself in potential. Any talk of "receiving" the Spirit would be a reversion to the language of an external force and Schleiermacher has made the Spirit itself immanent within human personality in order to avoid the pitfalls of dualism. When Schleiermacher writes of the universal potential for the Spirit, he seems to be saying that the Spirit itself is a potential in all men.

From the standpoint of Christ, then, the Spirit is divine. The Spirit is the communication of Christ's divine potency to men. From the human standpoint the Spirit is another name for a natural, human endowment—the potential of God-consciousness and the potential to enter into community. In his drive to locate the Holy Spirit in man as well as in Christ, Schleiermacher has lost some sense of the sovereignty of the Holy Spirit who "blows where he wills." He plays down, if he does not entirely reject, what the primitive church emphasized the most—that in the experience of the Spirit one has contact with the very life of God himself and not with another name for man's need for liberation or for community.

Schleiermacher, then, returns to some elements of the doctrine of the Spirit found in the church before the Trinitarian controversy. For dogmatic reasons, he revives the early church's limitation of the Spirit to the Christian community and its identification of the Spirit with Christ. He is thereby able to recapture the Pauline emphasis on the Spirit's belonging to and building up the community and to counteract the individualism inherent in some other views of the Spirit's work.

In Schleiermacher, the community provides the objectivity to the Spirit's work, which classical Trinitarian theology maintained by making the Spirit a part of the Godhead. In Schleiermacher, the transcendence of the Holy Spirit is the transcendence of the community to those who make it up. The Spirit is not transcendent to mankind as a whole. Rather the Spirit is a potential, a need, for fellowship within human personality. The work of the Spirit is the same as the fulfillment of this need. Schleiermacher maintains more forcefully than many theologians the close connection between the Spirit and the communal nature of the Body of Christ but his total reliance on psychological categories truncates the sovereignty and power of the Spirit by undermining the transcendent part of the Spirit's existence and function.

Notes

CHAPTER 1

1. The best general history of religious communities in America is Mark Holloway, *Heavens on Earth: Utopian Communities in America 1680-1880* (New York: Dover Publications, 1966). For background see Whitney Cross, *The Burned-Over District* (New York: Harper & Row, Torchbooks, 1965). More specific information is in Arthur Bestor, *Backwoods Utopia* (Philadelphia: University of Pennsylvania Press, 1967) and E. D. Andrews *The People Called Shakers* (New York: Dover Publications, 1963).

2. Good histories of the charismatic movement in America are available in Morton Kelsey, *Tongue Speaking* (Garden City: Doubleday, 1964); Michael Harper, *As at the Beginning* (Plainfield, N.J.: Logos Press, 1971); John L. Sherrill, *They Speak with Other Tongues* (Westwood, N.J.: Revell, 1964); and John T. Nichol, *Pentecostalism* (New York: Harper & Row, 1966). For the movement in the Roman Catholic Church see Kevin and Dorothy Ranaghan, *Catholic Pentecostals* (Paramus, N.J.: Paulist Press, 1969) and Edward D. O'Connor, *The Pentecostal Movement in the Catholic Church* (Notre Dame: Ave Maria Press, 1971). My own interpretation of the history of American Pentecostalism can be found in James Jones, *Filled with New Wine* (New York: Harper & Row, 1974).

3. This section of the book has put me happily in debt to many people: to the chroniclers of the communal movement of the sixties in America who have written innumerable articles everywhere, from the *New York Times* to the underground press, especially Robert Houriet, Dick Fairfield, and Consuel Sondoval; to Professor Frank Kirkpatrick of Trinity College, Hartford, Connecticut, who taught a seminar on modern communes and generously made available to me the material he used and the conclusions of his students; and

especially to all the people who shared freely and openly with me their own experiences and experiments in communal living.

4. Robert Houriet, *Getting Back Together* (New York: Coward, McCann and Geoghegan, 1971), pp. xii-xiii.

5. Ibid., p. xxxiv.

6. For example, Houriet, op. cit., or David French, "After the Fall," *New York Times Magazine*, Oct. 3, 1971, pp. 20ff.

7. The following discussion is heavily based on the brilliant analysis of the impact of psychology on our culture done by Philip Rieff and I am glad to acknowledge my debt to him. In his books, *Freud: The Mind of the Moralist* (Garden City: Doubleday, 1961) and *The Triumph of the Therapeutic* (New York: Harper & Row, 1966), Rieff argues that the popularization of psychoanalysis has produced a new social type whom he calls "psychological man" and a new social ethos, which he labels "therapeutic." Psychological man is ultimately concerned only about his own psychological process; the therapeutic ethos teaches him to regard all social forms, politics, religion, and art only as supports and enrichments of his psychic well-being.

8. Houriet, op. cit., p. 10.

9. This is the sentiment of Stephen Clark's book, *Building Christian Communities* (Notre Dame: Ave Maria Press, 1972).

10. Reported in Ralph Keyes, *We, The Lonely People* (New York: Harper & Row, 1973), p. 159.

11. Bertil Ghezzi, "Three Charismatic Communities," in Kevin and Dorothy Ranaghan, *As the Spirit Leads Us* (Paramus, N.J.: Paulist Press, 1971), p. 164.

12. Jones, *Filled with New Wine*, op. cit.; Clark, *Building Christian Communities*, op. cit.; Ranaghan, *As the Spirit Leads Us*, op. cit. For a more general discussion see Keyes, *We, The Lonely People*, op. cit.

CHAPTER 3

1. Calvin's thought is discussed in chapter 4; for Luther see Regin Prenter, *Spiritus Creator* (Philadelphia: Muhlenberg Press, 1953), chap. 2.

2. Michael Polanyi, *Personal Knowledge* (New York: Harper & Row, Torchbooks, 1958). To his work I am indebted for the term "communal verification." Polanyi's investigations deal almost exclusively with "communal verification" in the natural sciences; for a book that usefully broadens the issues by considering both science and religion, see Ian Barbour, *Myths, Models, and Paradigms* (New York: Harper & Row, 1974).

3. Thus pluralism becomes the major theological problem for today. If knowledge is communally relative, what if various communities disagree? One can attempt to appeal to a larger community that embraces all men. Often such larger communities, being more abstract and less sophisticated about the par-

ticular issue, are not helpful. Nor is it clear that there is any larger community, say, the community of all reasonable men. What constitutes good reasoning has been a philosophical quandary since Plato. There appears no way to get beyond the community-relative nature of our knowledge, although there may be principles and stances of openness and tolerance that allow communities to break down barriers or coexist with their differences. Any such relativistic-sounding doctrine has serious problems. Even the statement that our knowledge is community-relative is itself relative · to a community formed by certain philosophical and · social-scientific ideas. Thus, although the *forms* of our knowledge are community-relative, the *object* of that knowledge need not be. Scientific theories are the function of scientific communities built around common assumptions and perceptions, but that does not mean that the physical world they refer to is relative. Obviously it is not. In the same way theological theories are relative to the community out of whose experience they grow but that does not entail that God (the referent of these theories) is relative.

CHAPTER 4

1. Eduard Schweizer, "Spirit of God," from *Bible Key Words*, vol. 3 (London: Adam & Charles Black, 1960), pp. 41–45; Harvey H. Guthrie, *Wisdom and Canon* (Evanston: Seabury-Western Theological Seminary, 1966), chap. 2.

2. Schweizer, op. cit., and Neill Hamilton, *The Holy Spirit and Eschatology in St. Paul* (Edinburgh: Oliver & Boyd, 1957); *Scottish Journal of Theology* occasional papers no. 6, chaps. 2–3.

3. For example, Hans Lietzmann, *A History of the Early Church*, vol. I, trans. B. L. Woolf (Cleveland: World Pub. Co., Meridian Books, 1961), pt. 12.

4. "The Epistle of Ignatius to the Magnesians," in *The Ante-Nicene Fathers*, vol. 1, A. R. Roberts and J. Donaldson, eds. (Grand Rapids: W. B. Eerdmans, 1885), p. 65.

5. "Shepherd of Hermas," Similitude V, chap. 6, in *The Apostolic Fathers*, J. B. Lightfoot, ed. (London: Macmillan, 1912), p. 447.

6. Cf. Hendrikus Berkhof, *The Doctrine of the Holy Spirit* (London: Epworth Press, 1964), chap. 1.

7. Apology, 33, *The Ante-Nicene Fathers*, op. cit.

8. "Against Heresies," 4/20/3, from *The Ante-Nicene Fathers*, op. cit.

9. Cf. George S. Hendry, *The Holy Spirit in Christian Theology* (Philadelphia: The Westminster Press, 1956), p. 29.

10. "Against Heresies," 3/17/2, op. cit.

11. See L. G. Patterson, "The Conversion of 'Diastema' in the Patristic View of Time," *Lux in Lumine*, R. A. Norris, ed. (New York: Seabury Press, 1966).

12. "On the Holy Spirit," *The Nicene and Post-Nicene Fathers*, second series, P. Schaff and H. Wace, eds. (Grand Rapids, Mich.: W. B. Eerdmans [1892]).

13. Cf. George S. Hendry, op. cit., pp. 26–27, 29.

14. Cf. Lindsay Dewar, *The Holy Spirit and Modern Thought* (New York: Harper & Brothers, 1960), pt. 2.

15. *Summa Theologica* 3/4/42, from *Aquinas on Nature and Grace*, Library of Christian Classics, vol. 11 (Philadelphia: The Westminster Press, 1954).

16. Ibid. 2/1/109 A5.

17. Ibid. 2/1/114 A5.

18. Ibid. 2/1/109 A2.

19. *Summa Theologica* 2/1/62 A1.

20. Ibid. 2/1/68, Ab.

21. *Summa Contra Gentiles*, trans., English Dominican Fathers (London: Burns, Oates & Washbourne, Ltd, 1929) p. 423.

22. *Summa Theologica* 1/27/A3.

23. Economic views of the Trinity say that the Three Persons are distinguished solely by function and need not represent any actual divisions within the Godhead. Ontological Trinitarianism says that the Three Persons represent three structural divisions within the Godhead.

24. *Institutes of the Christian Religion*, trans., F. L. Battles, Library of Christian Classics, vols. 20-21 (Philadelphia: Westminster Press, 1960) 3/2/33.

25. Ibid.

26. Ibid., 1/7/5.

27. Ibid., 2/2/20.

28. Ibid.

29. Ibid.

30. Ibid., 3/2/33, Calvin writes, "It is not enough for the mind to be illuminated by the Spirit of God unless the heart is also strengthened and supported by his power."

31. Ibid., 3/2/36.

32. Ibid., 3/2/14, cf. Edward Dowey, *The Knowledge of God in Calvin's Theology* (New York: Columbia University Press, 1952), pp. 181–185.

33. Ibid.

34. *Institutes*, op. cit., 3/1/3.

35. Ibid.

36. Ibid., 3/1/1.

37. Heiko Oberman, *The Harvest of Medieval Theology* (Cambridge: Harvard University Press, 1963), chap. 9; J. B. Carol, *Mariology* (Milwaukee: The Bruce Publishing Company, 1955), vol. 1, pp. 281–309.

38. Oberman, op. cit., pp. 317–319.

39. *Institutes*, op. cit., 3/2/4.

40. Ibid., 4/17/10.

41. Ibid., 1/13/15.

42. Ibid., 1/13/14.

43. Ibid.

44. *The Christian Faith*, H. R. Mackintosh and J. S. Stewart, eds. (New York: Harper & Row, 1963), p. 570.

45. Ibid., p. 577.

46. Ibid., p. 575.

47. James D. G. Dunn, *Baptism in the Holy Spirit* (London: SCM Press, 1970). *Studies in Biblical Theology*, no. 15 argues against the Pentecostal and Holiness churches' teaching that conversion is followed by a "second blessing" of baptism in the Spirit. Rather, he says, the New Testament teaches that conversion, an experential Baptism in the Spirit with Spiritual gifts, and baptismal entrance into the church occur at the same time!

48. *Christian Faith*, op. cit, p. 571.

49. All the passages Schleiermacher singles out for rejection are from "Acts."

50. *Christian Faith*, op. cit., p. 572.

51. Ibid., p. 573.

Index

Index

Noyes, John Humphrey. *See* Oneida community

Objectivity, of knowledge, 95–98, 100–104
Oneida community, 20–21, 46
Origen, 117

Pentecost, Day of, 2, 8, 77
Pentecostal churches. *See also* Charismatic movement, 1, 22–27, 68–69, 93–95
Polanyi, Michael, 102

Rauschenbusch, Walter. *See* Social Gospel
Reiff, Philip, 33

St. Paul, 9–13, 38, 39, 47, 52, 60–61, 63, 67, 81, 86, 93–94, 95, 99–100, 111–112, 145, 147
Schleiermacher, F. D. E., 6, 83, 86, 90, 96–97, 138–151
Shakers, 19–20, 22, 46
Smith, Joseph. *See* Mormons
Social Gospel, 56–58, 62–64, 66–68
Spirit, Holy, and the church, 90–95, 119, 142–148; and community, 10–12, 13, 44–50, 67, 95–106; as divine love, 124–128; as divine volition, 125–128, 137–138; in God's plan, 10–12; and Kingdom of God, 58–59, 69; as mediator, 86–89, 134–136; and scripture, 95–106, 129–132; as sign of eschaton, 109–112; and the Son, 81–88, 114–119; as theological authority, 95–106; in wisdom tradition, 79–81, 108–112

Spiritual gifts, in Aquinas, 123; and community, 10–12, 44–48; and Kingdom, 59, 68, 74–76; in St. Paul, 9–13; in therapeutic communes, 33–36, 40, 47

Trinity, doctrine of, 71–72, 82, 90, 117–120, 125–128, 137, 146, 150–151

Wisdom, Divine, 79–80, 108–112, 116, 134–135